The Little of Stories from Around the World

by Marianne Sargent
Illustrations by Samantha Farina

LITTLE BOOKS WITH **BIG** IDEAS

Published 2010 by A&C Black Publishers Limited
36 Soho Square, London W1D 3QY
www.acblack.com

ISBN 978-1-4081-2327-0

Text © Marianne Sargent, 2010
Illustrations © Samantha Farina, Beehive Illustration 2010
Cover photographs © Shutterstock

Printed in Great Britain by Latimer Trend & Company Limited

This book is produced using paper that is made from wood grown in
managed, sustainable forests. It is natural, renewable and recyclable.

The logging and manufacturing processes conform to the environmental
regulations of the country of origin.

**To see our full range of titles
visit www.acblack.com**

Contents

Introduction

This book is aimed at practitioners working with young children in Foundation Stage settings as well as teachers working in Key Stage 1. It is intended as a resource to support the thematic use of traditional stories from around the world.

Stories from different countries

Stories are a powerful medium that engage and envelop young children, giving them the opportunity to enter imaginary worlds and meet a variety of characters. Stories from a range of countries allow children to travel into unfamiliar places, enabling them to experience alternative ways of life and encounter characters that hold different beliefs and traditions.

'Stories are a means of learning about life, emotion, culture and morals. History, culture and family experiences have been handed down the generations through traditions of storytelling... Experience of stories therefore helps everyone to understand the world in which we live, enabling us to make connections between what we are learning and what we already know.' (Brock and Rankin, 2008, Communication, Language and Literacy from Birth to Five, p.65.)

The Practice Guidance for the Early Years Foundation Stage sets out the requirement that children be provided with 'positive images that challenge children's thinking and help them embrace differences in gender, ethnicity, language, religion, culture...' (DCSF, 2008, PSED card). Traditional tales from other countries can be used as a springboard for learning about a variety of cultures and exploring difference. Choosing stories that celebrate the ethnicity of minorities within a setting, not only helps such children to feel valued and included, but encourages other children to respect and understand diversity. Furthermore, the cultural familiarity of such stories to those children who speak English as an additional language may stir an interest within them, potentially enhancing their learning experience.

'Children's backgrounds will obviously shape their experiences and should be taken into account, for example, by recognising cultural events, such as religious festivals and traditional stories. These can provide powerful learning opportunities to boost speaking, listening, reading and writing in English. (Rose Review, 2006, p.24)

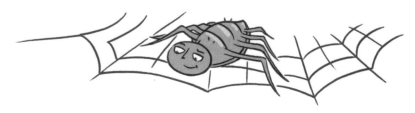

The storytelling tradition

Listening to stories is a fundamental part of early literacy development. Before children can begin to make sense of and understand the purpose of written language they must first become confident speakers and listeners. This is only possible in a literate environment where children are given ample opportunity to enjoy listening to spoken language and are actively encouraged to communicate.

'A child's ability to develop language depends on being immersed in a rich environment of words, sounds, rhythm, and verbal and non-verbal expression from birth.' (DCSF, 2008, Every Child a Talker, p.3)

Storytelling without the distraction of text and pictures encourages active listening. It also provides the teller with the opportunity to build in rhythm and repetition, offering children the chance to join in. Although each featured folktale, myth and legend has been published within this book for the benefit of practitioners, all are derived from oral origins, having been passed down between generations of storytellers throughout the centuries. These stories are intended to enable practitioners to exploit the benefits of storytelling.

Using the book

The book features fifteen stories from around the world. For each you will find:

▶ The story abridged and re-told for the benefit of the practitioner

▶ Suggested adult-led activities related to the story

▶ The relevant learning intentions covered in undertaking these activities

▶ A list of songs, rhymes and poems

▶ Suggested independent activities

▶ Some useful websites

▶ A list of additional stories and information books.

All of the suggested activities and resources for the featured stories are specific to the themes that arise in each. However, the use of multicultural stories offers many opportunities for learning across the six areas of learning and development and below is a number of suggestions for generic activities that can be applied to each story.

Generic activities

▶ Locate the featured country on a map or globe and look at its flag.

▶ Use information books, photographs, CD-ROMS and the Internet to find out about the way of life for those living in each country. You could look at: Weather and climate; architecture and housing; clothing; agriculture and food; currency and stamps; religions, customs and beliefs; vehicles and transport.

▶ Find out how to say hello and goodbye in each language.

▶ Find out about the local wildlife: Find out which are the largest/smallest, strongest/weakest and fastest/slowest; encourage the children to move and make sounds like different animals; play listening games – match the sound to the animal.

▶ Examine local artefacts and encourage the children to verbally describe them.

▶ Play music from each country and examine musical instruments from different cultures: Ask the children to describe the sounds that they hear; watch examples of people from different cultures dancing; dance to the music; provide instruments so that the children can compose music of their own.

▶ Retell the story verbally, with the use of puppets or a storyboard.

▶ Think of alternative plots, events and story endings.

▶ Suggest alternatives for main characters.

▶ Use a computer presentation program, e.g. PowerPoint to make an interactive electronic storybook.

▶ Look at typical modes of transport to each featured country.

▶ Role-play settings might include: Travel agent; aeroplane; passenger ferry; hotel; restaurants serving a variety of ethnic foods.

General areas of learning and development covered through the use of multicultural stories

Personal, social and emotional development:

- ▶ Have an awareness of, and an interest in, cultural and religious differences.
- ▶ Understand that people have different needs, views, cultures and beliefs, that need to be treated with respect.

Communication, language and literacy:

- ▶ Listen to and join in with stories and poems, one-to-one and also in small groups.
- ▶ Describe main story settings, events and principal characters.
- ▶ Use a widening range of words to express or elaborate on ideas.
- ▶ Explore and experiment with texts.
- ▶ Retell narratives in the correct sequence, drawing on the language pattern of stories.
- ▶ Show an understanding of the elements of stories, such as main character, sequence of events and openings, and how information can be found in non-fiction texts to answer questions about where, who, why and how.

Knowledge and understanding of the world:

- ▶ Find out about, and identify, some features of living things, objects and events they observe.
- ▶ Find out about the use of information and communication technology – CD-ROMS and the Internet.
- ▶ Begin to differentiate between past and present.
- ▶ Show an interest in the world in which they live.
- ▶ Observe, find out about and identify features in the place they live and the natural world.
- ▶ Show interest in different occupations and ways of life.
- ▶ Begin to know about their own cultures and beliefs and those of other people.
- ▶ Use a mouse and a keyboard to interact with computer software.

Creative development:

- ▶ Imitate and create movement in response to music.
- ▶ Explore the different sounds of instruments.
- ▶ Engage in imaginative play and role-play based on own firsthand experiences.

Elephant, Hare and Hippo

Southeast Africa

The hot African sun bore down upon the elephant as he flapped his enormous ears to shoo away the flies and dust. Through the bushes he could see the hippo basking in the coolness of the watering hole, lazily kicking his legs and splashing around. The elephant thought how wonderful it would be if the hippo would agree to share his bath and allow the elephant to cool himself in the water. So he went to him and pleaded,

'Hippo dear friend, would you mind if I joined you?'

The hippo peered up at him and lazily replied,

'You are no friend of mine. Go and find your own watering hole.'

The hot sun continued to bear down on the elephant's neck and he blinked as the dust stung his eyes. He flapped his ears crossly and shouted at the hippo, 'Then never again come to graze near my home!'

Raising his trunk high, he turned his back on the hippo and stomped up the bank and back through the bushes.

A hare, hiding in some tall grasses nearby heard the argument and deciding that he should put an end to it, ran down to the water and called out to the Hippo.

'Hey you there! I bet I am stronger than you!' 'Come out of the water and test your strength against me.'

The hippo laughed again. He knew this was ridiculous but he was bored and thought it would be fun to tease the hare. Once out of the water he allowed the hare to tie a rope around his waist.

The hare said, 'I will take the other end of this rope through those bushes. When you feel me tug, start to pull and we will see who is the strongest.'

The hare bounded out of sight through the bushes where he found the elephant sulking on the other side.

'Hey you there!' he shouted. 'I bet I am stronger than you!'

This cheered up the elephant no end and he laughed out loud, flapping his ears and stamping his feet. The hare stood tall and pushed out his chest.

'I bet I am stronger than you and I can prove it with a game.'

The elephant looked down at him with a smile. A game couldn't do any harm; after all it might take his mind off the heat and the sun. He allowed the hare to tie a rope around his waist and watched as the hare bounded off into the bushes, while he waited to start pulling.

Hidden in the bushes, the hare took hold of the middle of the rope and gave it a pull in each direction, first against the hippo, then against the elephant. Feeling the tug, each massive, powerful animal began to pull against the other, while the hare lay back in the bushes and waited. The hippo and the elephant pulled against each other for hours. As the sun went down and the moon appeared in the sky the elephant was so tired that his legs gave way and he collapsed in a heap. The rope slackened and the Hippo lost his balance, tipped forward and tumbled into the watering hole with an enormous splash.

Hearing the noise, the elephant ran to the water, stretched out his trunk and helped the hippo out onto the bank. Feeling foolish that such a small creature as the hare had tricked them, they made friends again and decided that from then on they would share the watering hole and graze together in peace.

Adult-led activities to follow up the story

▶ Discuss the story – ask the children why they think the hare tricked the hippo and the elephant. Talk about sharing and being kind.

▶ Discuss why water is so important for people, animals and plants to stay alive.

▶ Explain that in some areas of the world clean water is scarce and consider the implications of this. (Find more information about this on the WaterAid website at **www.wateraid.org/uk**.)

▶ Experiment with growing plants; give them different amounts of water and observe what happens.

▶ Show the children pictures of different African animals; ask children to move like each animal considering its shape, size and speed.

▶ Investigate a selection of ropes and strings: discuss their purposes; test their strengths; dip them in paint to print patterns.

▶ Experiment with forces by tying weighted objects to string and pulling them through a range of substances, e.g. pulling a kilogram weight through dry sand, rice, water and slime. Discuss and compare ease/difficulty experienced.

Independent activities

▶ Display photographs and posters of wild African animals in the art area as inspiration for the children to draw or paint pictures or make playdough/junk models.

▶ Set up an obstacle course in the outdoor area that requires the children to jump over obstacles like hares.

▶ Provide a set of sorting animals for children to sort according to size.

▶ Set up a small world story scene in the sand tray with a bowl of water, plastic toy animals and string.

Songs, rhymes and poems

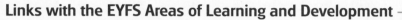

I turn on the tap/I walk to the stream

Find this song on the Internet at **www.singup.org**.

The Elephant – by Hilaire Belloc.

Find this poem on the Internet at **www.thepoemhunter.com**

Elephant – Anon.

Find this poem in Elephants and Emus and Other Animal Rhymes by Philippa-Alys Browne.

Links with the EYFS Areas of Learning and Development

PSED – understand that there needs to be agreed values and codes of behaviour for groups of people to work together harmoniously.

KUW – show understanding of cause/effect relations – water and life; investigate materials by using all of their senses as appropriate; ask questions about why things happen and how things work.

PD – recognise the importance of keeping healthy and how water consumption contributes to this.

CD – understand that different media can be combined to create new effects.

More stories and information

Clever Tortoise by Francesca Martin – a variation on the Hare, Hippo and Tortoise.

Tricky Tortoise by Mwenye Hadithi and Adrienne Kennaway – another variation on the same tale.

Elmer and the Hippos by David McKee – lovely story about how the elephants and hippos work together so that they can all enjoy the river water.

The Hare by Jill Mason and David Mason – adult's information book about hares from Europe, America and Africa with very good photographs.

Elephants: A Book for Children by Steve Bloom – children's information book with excellent photographs.

African Wildlife Foundation website – for photos, general information and animal sounds go to **www.awf.org/section/wildlife/gallery**

King Midas

Ancient Greece

King Midas of Pessinus quietly sneaked along a hidden passageway that led down to the underground chambers of his castle. Stowed away in a dingy little secret room that only Midas had a key for, were his many riches; piles of gold and silver coins, diamond jewellery and golden goblets encrusted with precious stones.

After spending many hours counting his coins and admiring his jewels, Midas locked up his little room and ventured out into the castle grounds. He wandered out into the sunshine and strode around his rose garden daydreaming. He looked at the daffodils and imagined they were dripping in amber; he turned to the tulips and dreamt they were scarlet cups of rubies; and he marveled at the pond as it appeared to ripple with liquid silver.

All of a sudden Midas was surprised to notice a pair of shoes poking out from under a bush. On closer inspection he found that the shoes belonged to a man who was quietly snoozing in the shade. Midas poked the man with a branch, awaking him with a start.

'Who are you and what are you doing sleeping in my rose bushes?' Midas scorned.

The man quickly pulled himself to his feet. He brushed down his clothes and picked twigs out of his wiry grey hair. 'I am Silenus, foster father of the great god Dionysus,' he declared. 'I have been walking for days in the heat and needed somewhere to rest.' Midas knew that the mighty Dionysus had been looking for

Silenus since he had gone missing several days earlier.

He quickly realised that returning Silenus to Dionysus could earn him a hefty reward. 'Of course! Dionysus has been going crazy worrying about you,' he said. 'I will take you back to him. But first you must stay in my castle and build up your strength so that you return fit and well.'

Silenus enjoyed the King's hospitality for ten days. He bathed in the castle's lavish bathrooms, feasted at generous banquets and drank the King's finest wine. By the eleventh day Silenus was looking healthy again and Midas decided it was time for him to return home.

'My father, my dear father!' Dionysus cried out. 'Not only have you been returned to me, but you look better than ever before!'

Silenus explained how Midas had generously welcomed and helped him.

'So you are the man I must thank,' Dionysus said to Midas. 'I shall reward you for your compassion by granting you a wish.'

Midas had been hoping this would happen and had been considering his reward the whole time Silenus had been staying with him. Without hesitation he said, 'I wish for everything I touch to be changed into gold.'

Dionysus was surprised and warned Midas that this could only bring him unhappiness. The King was adamant however, and so Dionysus granted his wish. Midas was delighted.

On his way back home he touched the branch of an oak tree and watched in disbelief as it turned into solid gold. He then bent down and picked up a stone, transforming it into a golden nugget. Back at the castle he ordered the servants to prepare a celebratory banquet and he invited his daughter Marigold to join him.

'Rejoice, dear Marigold. I have a new gift to share with you,' Midas cried.

He picked up a yellow rose and held it out to her. She gasped and looked at him in disbelief as it slowly became rigid and began to sparkle in the candlelight.

'Eat, dear Marigold. This is a celebration,' he said grabbing a chicken leg and leaning in to take a bite.But before the meat had reached his mouth it had become rock solid.

The King dropped the leg onto his plate and picked up a bread roll. This also turned to gold. Midas looked at Marigold in despair. He took up his goblet of wine and raised it to his lips, only to find that it too had turned into liquid gold.

'I cannot eat or drink,' he exclaimed. 'I shall die of thirst and starvation!'

Midas stood up, knocking his chair over in a panic, ran to his daughter and took hold of her hand.

'What must I do, dear Marigold?' he cried. To his horror, before she could reply, his little Marigold's face froze. Her skin became the colour of gold and all she could do was stand before him like a statue.

Blinded by the glitter of gold King Midas had gotten more than he bargained for.

Adult-led activities to follow up the story

▶ Discuss the story – ask the children why Midas was foolish to wish as he did. Talk about greed.

▶ Look at some examples of Ancient Greek architecture, e.g. the Parthenon and the Colosseum: Consider how these buildings have become ruined over time; make junk models and cover them with mod-roc or plaster of Paris.

▶ Make a treasure trove; use junk and shiny materials, e.g. gold and silver paper, tinfoil, coloured cellophane, glitter, sequins and glass pebbles to create jewels and items of treasure.

▶ Find out about the value of gold. Compare gold with other precious metals – examine some samples. Find out what they are used for and why they are so expensive.

▶ Find out about gold mining. Set up a role play gold mine; make fake gold nuggets by spray painting stones, hide them in trays of soil/sand and provide digging tools and sieves. Provide scales for children to weigh their find. Provide a simple chart showing how much each amount is worth, e.g. 1 gram = £1.

▶ Set up a treasure hunt using simple directional and positional clue cards. Invite the children to contribute to a class treasure trove of precious personal items. Ask them to describe their objects and explain their significance.

Independent activities

▶ Use the jewels and treasure made by the children for a role-play jewellers store or King Midas' treasure trove.

▶ Set up a small world gold mine – available from Playmobil.

▶ Set up a mini Olympics stadium in the outdoor area with a racetrack, obstacle course, target ball/beanbag games and medals.

▶ Do a large-scale splatter painting outside with various shades of gold and yellow paint.

Songs, rhymes and poems

If Only I Had Plenty of Money – by Paul Edmonds.
Find this poem in the Hutchinson Treasury of Children's Poetry.

The Dollar Song
Find this poem on the Internet at **www.earlyliterature.ecsd.net/math.htm**

Mega Greek Myth Raps – by Tony Mitton and Martin Chatterton.
This book features the story of King Midas in rhyming rap form and is published by Orchard Books.

Links with the EYFS Areas of Learning and Development

PSED – Value and contribute to own well-being and self-control; consider the consequences of their words and actions for themselves and others.

CLL – Speak clearly and audibly with confidence and control and show awareness of the listener.

PSRN – Begin to make comparisons between quantities; find items from positional or directional clues.

KUW – Develop an understanding of decay and changes over time; begin to differentiate between past and present; investigate objects and materials using all of their senses as appropriate.

PD – Engage in activities requiring hand-eye coordination.

CD – Create constructions using junk and mod-roc; explore colour, texture, form and shape in three dimensions.

More stories and information

King Midas's Goldfingers (First Greek Myths) by Saviour Pirotta and Jan Lewis – a simple retelling.

King Midas and the Golden Touch by Charlotte Craft and K. Y. Craft – a lengthier version with background information.

Usborne Greek Myths for Young Children by Heather Amery and Linda Edwards – an illustrated collection of myths retold for younger children.

Rumpelstiltskin by Margaret Mayo and Selina Young – a well-known traditional tale about a king's greed for gold.

The Greeks: Activities, Crafts, History by Sally Hewitt – a simple information book providing an overview of Ancient Greek life.

Gold Fever by Verla Kay and S. D. Schindler – a picture book with rhyming text about the Californian gold rush.

The Little Koala and the Bunyip

Australia

For hundreds of years Australians warned their children to stay away from the creeks and billabongs for fear of the mighty bunyip. The Aborigine people were so frightened of this monster that they would only ever travel to the watering hole in large groups.

One creature that was not afraid of the bunyip was a little koala bear who lived at the top of a mountain. Each night she would tuck her baby in to sleep and run down to the bottom of the mountain to drink from the creek.

On one particular night as the little koala drank, the water of the creek began to ripple. She lifted her head and peered out into the deepest part, where the ripple was curling into a wave and the most grotesque creature she had ever seen was emerging. It had the face of a dog, but with a huge snout and enormous tusks that stuck out and glistened in the moonlight. The little koala did not move, but just sat at the side of the creek and watched as the monster dragged itself towards her using its four bulky flipper like legs.

'You must be the mighty bunyip,' she said, craning her neck to look up at his hairy face.

The bunyip looked down curiously at the little bear that seemed so unafraid of him. He was used to people and animals running away from him in terror.

'You are not scared!' he said in amazement. 'Why should I be scared of you? I have been drinking at this creek for many years and you have never hurt me before now,' the koala replied. 'In fact, I should like to invite you to my home. I believe we could be friends.'

The bunyip was so surprised and delighted at this show of friendship that he gladly accepted the invitation and followed the little koala up the mountain to her home. She prepared a midnight snack for the bunyip and they sat talking, laughing and eating into the small hours.

Unfortunately, the bunyip's flippers were meant for traveling through water and this made him a clumsy climber, knocking down trees and sending boulders crashing as he scrambled up and down the mountain. The following day the other koalas noticed this trail of destruction and were terribly unhappy to find out about the new friendship.

They knew the Aborigine people were terrified of the bunyip. They were afraid that if the Aborigines found out a koala had made friends with a bunyip, they would grow to hate koalas and start hunting them for food. They resolved that the friendship must end.

The elder koalas suggested that they capture the magic of the featherfoot, an enchanted creature that had patterns all over its body.

'The magic is in the markings,' one of the elders explained. 'If we use clay to copy the pattern onto my body I will then have the same powers.'

As night approached, the elder koala, painted in clay, hid in the trees by the little koala's home and watched while she tucked her baby into bed. As she ran down the mountain toward the creek, the elder koala grabbed the baby, ran after her and dropped him onto the little koala's back whispering 'Hang on tight and never let go.'

The featherfoot's magic worked. The baby clung on as tight as he could and no matter what she tried, the little koala could not shrug him off. Instead of visiting her new friend the bunyip she had to return home.

The bunyip waited at the edge of the creek all night. As the sun began to rise he finally gave up and hanging his head with sorrow he pulled himself back into the creek and dove down into its depths.

When the little koala awoke the next day she found a large gathering outside her home. She looked at the elder koala, who was standing at the front painted in clay.

'Why are you all here and what has happened to your face?' **she asked.**

'You will no longer be friends with the bunyip,' **the elder koala said.** 'To make sure you never visit the creek again, your baby will forever cling to your back. What's more,' **he continued,** 'the marks on my face will appear on those of all koalas to serve as a reminder to all that the bunyip is dangerous. He is not our friend and never will be.'

Adult-led activities to follow up the story

▶ Discuss the story – ask the children how the bunyip might feel about being alone. Why was everyone so scared of the bunyip? Talk about difference, acceptance and friendship.

▶ Circle time – I like you because... Ask the children to think of something nice to say about the child next to them or roll a ball to a child of their choice.

▶ Talk about mythical creatures and show some examples, e.g. dragons, ogres, the phoenix, the Scottish Loch Ness Monster. Challenge the children to make up their own mythical creatures and draw/paint them, make models of them with clay, dough or junk and think of adjectives to describe them.

▶ Play 'That's What They Call the Didgeridoo' by Rolf Harris. Show the children a real didgeridoo or pictures. Make mini didgeridoos by decorating kitchen rolls.

▶ Make cardboard cut out koalas. (Find a template and instructions at **www.dltk-kids.com/animals/mkoala2.htm.**)

Independent activities

▶ Display Aboriginal artwork in the art area for inspiration.

▶ Provide photocopied templates of Aboriginal designs and patterns. (Find these in Aboriginal Designs by Penny Brown, available from Search Press.)

▶ Provide cotton buds and paint for children to recreate Aboriginal art.

▶ Set up a role-play expedition camp. Provide explorer outfits and equipment such as binoculars, magnifying glasses, compasses and torches for children to hunt for mythical creatures.

▶ Ask the children to create a small world land for toy mythical creatures.

Songs, rhymes and poems

I Often Meet a Monster – by Max Fatchen.
Find this poem in the Oxford Treasury of Children's Poems.

What Does a Bunyip Look Like – by Francis Duggan.
Find this poem on the Internet at **www.thepoemhunter.com**

Koala Is Not a Bear
Find this poem on the Internet at:
www.teapartydiva.com/koala-is-not-a-bear-kids-tea-party-poem

Links with the EYFS Areas of Learning and Development

PSED – Be caring towards each other; form friendships with other children; show care and concern for others; be sensitive to the feelings of others.

CLL – Use a widening range of words to express ideas; use talk to organise, sequence and clarify thinking and ideas.

KUW – Investigate objects and materials by using all of their senses as appropriate.

CD – Use language and other forms of communication to share the things they create; create 3D craft models, paintings and drawings; show an interest in the way that musical instruments sound.

More stories and information

The Bunyip of Berkeley's Creek by Jenny Wagner and Ron Brooks – a bunyip is disappointed to be told he is ugly by the other animals in the Bush.

An Australian ABC of Animals by Bronwyn Bancroft – beautifully illustrated by an Aboriginal artist.

Koala Lou by Mem Fox and P. Lofts – a baby koala tries to impress his mum by competing in the Bush Olympics.

Stories from the Billabong by James Vance Marshall and Francis Firebrace – ten illustrated Aboriginal legends.

Tusk Tusk by David McKee – a story about difference and prejudice.

Australian Wildlife (Nature Kids) by Pat Slater – an overview of unusual Australian wildlife with colour photographs.

The National Library of Australia website – for animated bunyip tales, educational activities and games go to:
www.nla.gov.au/exhibitions/bunyips/flash-site/index-flash.html

Paraparawa and Waraku

Amazonian Rainforest, Brazil

In the beginning the Trio people of Brazil lived out in the open with just the canopy of the rainforest to shelter them. At this time the tribe survived by eating wild grasses and reeds as well as any fruits and berries they could find. Sometimes they would be lucky enough to enjoy some fresh juicy fish from the nearby River Amazon.

Unfortunately, the food did not last long in any one area and the tribe often had to move on and find new places to live, where fresh fruit hung from the trees and new berries grew in the bushes. However, one particular morning Paraparawa the fisherman discovered something that was to change the fortunes of the Trio people forever.

'I've got you, I've got you, I've got you,' Paraparawa muttered as he grappled with a small round fish in the water. With a deft flick he flipped the fish onto the riverbank where it wriggled and writhed about gasping for air.

'A great start to the day,' he declared and he turned his back on the fish to scan the water for more. He stood absolutely still, careful not to make a sound. He was concentrating so hard that when a woman's voice suddenly broke the silence around him, he almost fell in the water.

'There is no need for more,' she said.

Paraparawa spun around to see a mysterious tall woman standing on the bank where the little round fish had been. 'I am the spirit of the fish you just caught,' she said. 'My name is Waraku.'

Paraparawa just stood staring in amazement. He couldn't believe his eyes.

'Take me to your home,' Waraku said. 'Show me how you and your tribe live.'

Paraparawa led Waraku to his tribe and explained that they lived a very simple life. They did not live in huts, but slept on beds of reeds. They did not have very much to eat, just the fruits of the plants around them. Waraku nodded and took Paraparawa back down to the river.

Standing on the riverbank, Waraku raised her arms, closed her eyes and cried out in a language Paraparawa had never heard before. A huge wave formed and came rushing toward them carrying an enormous alligator with a wide-open jaw.

'This is my father,' said Waraku, as the alligator stepped onto the bank and dropped a mouthful of strange looking objects onto the ground. He nodded at Waraku, turned and slid back into the water.

'I called to my father and asked him to bring you some food. Here we have some yams, sweet potatoes and bananas,' Waraku said, pointing to each and then turning to a strange looking plant. 'This is a yucca. You can eat the root and drink its juices,' she explained.

'Thank you,' Paraparawa said, 'but I have never seen anything like this before. How do we eat these and where do I find more?' he asked.

'You do not eat these,' Waraku replied. 'The idea is to plant them and grow more.'

Waraku showed Paraparawa how to clear enough space to make a field. She showed him how to plough the earth and helped him to plant the yams, sweet potatoes, bananas and yuccas in rows. She explained that the sun and the rain would help the plants to grow and before long the Trio tribe would have many fruits and vegetables to eat.

Paraparawa thanked Waraku again. She left and promised to come back when the crops were fully-grown. Over the coming weeks, Paraparawa tended his field each day and awaited the return of the spirit.

Finally one morning, Paraparawa arrived at the field to find Waraku wandering amongst the grown crops. She waved her hands around her and clapped with satisfaction at what they had achieved. Waraku explained that they should only harvest some of the food and keep the rest aside to plant and grow more. She then took Paraparawa to his tribe and showed them how to make tools for cooking and eating.

The Trio people continued to grow their own crops and no longer needing to move around, they built huts. They were extremely grateful for Waraku's help and never had to eat grasses and reeds again.

Adult-led activities to follow up the story

▶ Discuss the story – ask the children why it was so important for the Trio people to learn how to grow their own food.

▶ Discuss where we get our food from; look at the difference between supermarkets, green grocers, butchers, bakeries and markets.

▶ Investigate where our food is produced; local farms, factories, imports from abroad.

▶ Visit a food outlet or producer (as above).

▶ Involve the children in developing a small allotment; use window boxes and large planters if you do not have much space.

▶ Invite the children to taste yams and sweet potatoes; Yams can be roasted or grilled with olive oil; sweet potatoes can be baked and served with feta cheese.

▶ Make banana splits or exotic fruit salads.

▶ Find out about the Amazon rainforest; learn about its destruction and the environmental consequences.

▶ Make some recycled paper (find instructions on the Internet at **www.ecokids. ca/pub/fun_n_games/printables/activities/assets/science_nature/paper_ making.pdf**); use the paper to make save the rainforest posters.

Independent activities

▶ Vegetable printing with yams and sweet potatoes and ready-mixed paint.

▶ Role-play allotment outside with real gardening equipment, soil, seeds and plants.

▶ Role-play food market with real fruit and vegetables.

▶ Play rainforest sounds and music in a quiet area of the setting (available from Natural Sounds and TTS Group). Provide a range of musical instruments for children to respond with their own music.

Songs, rhymes and poems

Rainforest Animals – by Paul Hess.
This compilation of poems for young children is published by Zero to Ten.

Alligator – by Grace Nichols.
Find this poem in the Hutchinson Treasury of Children's Poetry.

Hippety Hop to the Corner Shop – by Elizabeth Matterson.
Find this song in This Little Puffin published by Puffin Books.

Links with the EYFS Areas of Learning and Development

PSED – Consider the consequences of their actions for themselves and others; be confident to try new vegetables and fruits; express likes and dislikes.

CLL – Use writing as a means of communicating; attempt writing for different purposes, using features of different forms such as persuasive posters.

KUW – Ask questions about why things happen and how things work; look closely at similarities and differences; show curiosity and interest in the features of living things; develop an understanding of growth over time; show understanding of cause/effect relations; use simple tools and techniques competently and appropriately.

More stories and information

Stories from the Amazon by Saviour Pirotta – an illustrated compilation of tales from Amazonian tribes people.

The Great Kapok Tree by Lynne Cherry – another Amazonian tale.

Make Your Own Rainforest by Clare Beaton – includes a pop up rainforest scene and facts about deforestation.

Big Farm Machines by Chronicle Books and Caterpillar – although this is a board book it has very good photographs of large farm machinery at work.

The Ant and the Grasshopper by Katie Daynes and Merel Eyckerman – a very simple version of Aesop's fable. Grasshopper is too lazy to harvest the food he needs to survive for the winter.

The Prince's Rainforest Project for Schools website – for information about rainforest conservation, lesson plans, assembly ideas and resources go to
http://schools.rainforestsos.org

The Twelve Wild Geese

Ireland

Once there was a king and queen who lived in a majestic castle and ruled over a beautiful green land. They were lucky enough to have twelve sons who had grown up to become fine young princes. But despite all they had the queen was desperately unhappy because all her life she had only ever wanted a daughter.

One day she cried out, 'If only I could have a daughter, I would trade all my sons for a little girl!' Suddenly there was a puff of smoke and a withered old witch appeared in front of her.

'You should be careful what you wish for my dear,' she cackled. 'You shall have a daughter and on the day that she is born all of your sons will disappear.'

The witch vanished. Everything happened just as she said. The queen did indeed have a baby girl and on the day she was born all twelve princes turned into a gaggle of geese and flew out of the castle windows and into the forest.

As the princess grew up she was told stories of her twelve brothers who had been turned into wild birds. These stories upset her so much that when she was twelve years old she left the castle and ventured into the forest to find them. Hidden amongst the trees she found a log cabin. She peered through the windows to see, a large dining table with twelve chairs around it. On the table were twelve plates, twelve cups and twelve knives and forks. She knew this was where she would find her brothers so she sat on the doorstep and waited. As the shadows around her began to lengthen twelve geese came swooping down from the blackening sky. Each big bird turned into a prince as his feet touched the ground. The princess leapt up in joy and ran to her brothers.

'I have found you alive! Now you must come back with me to the palace.'

At that moment the witch appeared. 'I don't think so!' she screeched. 'If you want your brothers to be free, you must work.'

She told the princess that she must collect enough bog cotton to weave twelve shirts. This would take her five years and during this time she was not to talk, laugh or cry.

For three years the princess did what the witch had told her. Then one day as she was making a start on the ninth shirt, a king from another kingdom came cantering though the forest on his horse.

'I have never seen a girl as enchanting as you. Come back with me and be my queen,' he declared.

The princess had been desperately unhappy spinning cotton day after day, unable to speak to her brothers and share in their jokes. She could go with the king and still make the shirts. Careful not to smile or speak, she grabbed her basket of cotton and her knitting basket and jumped on the back of the king's horse.

The princess lived happily with the king for the next two years, all the time making her brothers' shirts. The king did not mind that she never spoke or laughed. He knew that she was happy. On the day that their first child was born the witch reappeared.

She knew the princess was knitting her last shirt and soon her brothers would be free. Her only hope was to make her cry. She took the baby from the princess' arms and threw it out of the window into the jaws of a white wolf that ran with the baby into the forest. The princess was horrified but could not call out or cry. She knew the castle guards would be coming to arrest her and the king would think she had thrown their baby to the wolf.

As she was cast into the dungeons, she frantically continued to knit the last shirt. The very moment the barred door slammed she finally finished and shouted out loud,

'Brothers come to me now and take your shirts!'

The twelve geese came diving into the dungeon and the princess flung each of the twelve cotton shirts onto their backs. One by one they turned back into princes and tackled the guards to rescue their sister. At the same time a white witch appeared holding a baby in her arms. The princess cried for joy and thanked the good witch who had saved her baby disguised as a wolf.

Adult-led activities to follow up the story

▶ Discuss the story – ask the children to think about what happened to the queen when she made her wish. Talk about feelings of envy and jealousy and how it feels to want something you cannot have. How do we deal with these feelings?

▶ Help children design and decorate their own shirt. Use old children's shirts; tie-dye them, create patterns with fabric paints and pens, trim shaped hems with fabric scissors.

▶ Encourage the children to collect feathers for an interactive display where they match feathers to pictures of different birds.

▶ Find out about peatlands and bogs. Create a bog; fill a large shallow container with soil, old leaves and grass and soak in water. Provide magnifiers and pipettes, for the children to observe what happens as it goes stagnant, begins to smell and attract insects. Encourage volunteers to report back to the group each day.

▶ Find out the difference between geese and ducks. Visit a park and feed the ducks and geese.

▶ Make bog jelly; mix green and brown jelly with jelly creatures and bug sweets.

Independent activities

▶ Set up a role-play castle – provide dressing up clothes for kings, queens, princes and princesses; twelve different shirts; children's knitting needles and wool.

▶ Create collages with feathers of different shapes, colours and sizes.

▶ Use feathers and watercolours to paint and print patterns.

▶ Set up a small world story scenario with a castle, toy characters and geese.

▶ Create large-scale patterns on huge pieces of paper outdoors with muddy Wellington boot prints.

Songs, rhymes and poems

Goosey Goosey Gander
Find different versions of this traditional nursery rhyme in
The Oxford Dictionary of Nursery Rhymes.

Mudlarks – by Shirley Hughes
Find this poem in Olly and Me Out and About published by Walker Books.

Grey Goose
Find this traditional short poem in the Hutchinson Treasury of Children's Poetry.

Links with the EYFS Areas of Learning and Development

PSED – Express feelings in appropriate ways; have a developing awareness of their own feelings; are aware that some actions can hurt or harm others.

CLL – Speak clearly and audibly with confidence and control and show awareness of the listener.

KUW – Use simple tools and techniques competently and appropriately; show curiosity and interest in the features of living things; describe and talk about what they see; Look closely at similarities, differences, patterns and change.

CD – Understand that different media, e.g. dye, fabric paint and pens, can be combined to create new effects.

More stories and information

The Twelve Wild Geese by Matt Faulkner – one of the only versions in picture book form for children.

Tales from Old Ireland by Malachy Doyle and Niamh Sharkey – find another version of the tale in this beautifully illustrated compilation.

Borka: The Adventures of a Goose with No Feathers by John Burningham – a lovely heart-warming story.

The Bog Baby by Jeanne Willis and Gwen Millward – a little girl finds a strange creature in a pond.

S is for Shamrock by Eve Bunting and Matt Faulkner – an alphabet tour of Ireland.

Northern Ireland Environment and Heritage Service Peatlands website – for information about how peatlands and bogs are created and what grows in them go to **www.peatlandsni.gov.uk**

Qasiagssaq, The Great Liar

North America

Qasiagssaq opened the door of his hut and winced as the wind whipped across his face. He pulled his raven skin coat around him and stepped out into the freezing rain. He was late again. The rest of the men from the village were waiting impatiently outside, stamping their feet to keep warm.

'Why must we go out in the worst of weathers to hunt?' he whined.

Qasiagssaq was the laziest of all the Inuit men in his village. While the others worked hard to provide fish and seal meat for their families, he put all his effort into finding ways to avoid the toil of the hunt. He very rarely caught anything and often returned home with nothing except a couple of bony ravens.

Despite his laziness, Qasiagssaq's wife thought the best of him. She had no idea that when he did bring back something worthwhile, it had either been given to him or stolen from another hunter.

'Just do your best,' she said. 'You know I will be happy with whatever you bring home.'

He shrugged and stomped off through the snow to join up with the rest of the hunters, who were not so trusting. They knew Qasiagssaq was a liar and a cheat and had caught him on a number of occasions. Sometimes he had simply stolen their seals. Other times he had deliberately broken his harpoon so he couldn't hunt and they would have to share their catch with him.

On this particular day, they were out hunting for seal. After just an hour out at sea, Qasiagssaq was fed up. 'What is the point?' he complained. 'I never catch anything. I need to think of a way to make the other men share their catch with me.'

Then he had an idea. While the others paddled further out to sea, Qasiagssaq turned towards a nearby island and headed for a rocky section of coastline. His wooden kayak crunched onto the rocks, gouging a big hole in the side. Unaware that a woman picking berries nearby was watching him, he jumped out onto the shore, stripped off his clothes and battered them with his harpoon until they were ripped and tattered. He then took a fishing hook and scratched his arms until they bled, before picking up a heavy boulder and dropping it on his foot. Finally, he grabbed some chips of ice and stuffed them into his clothes. Crying in pain, he returned to his village, claiming he had hit an iceberg.

'My poor husband!' his wife cried and she bathed his wounds, strapped up his foot and tucked him into bed.

The villagers felt so sorry about his misfortune that they all rallied around to help. The men built him a new kayak and the women made him presents and took him food each day.

After a couple of weeks, Qasiagssaq was beginning to feel better. The villagers decided to throw a party and invited their neighbours over from the nearby islands. It was a fantastic party and it seemed as though all had been forgotten about Qasiagssaq's lies. Many believed that he had changed and everything would be different from now on.

Unfortunately for Qasiagssaq, it was not long before the woman from the island where he had wrecked his kayak recognised him and told everyone how she had seen him beating himself! The villagers were furious. They chased him into his hut, took back all their presents and told him never to speak to them again.

After many months spent alone and unhappy, Qasiagssaq decided he needed to win back the friendship of the villagers. He had an idea; he would tempt them with the promise of food.

'I have seen a dead whale on an island nearby,' he lied. 'It has enough meat on it for the whole village. If you allow me to join your hunt, I will show you where it is.'

The men were very suspicious of Qasiagssaq's claim, but wanted the meat for their families.

'Alright, we will give you one more chance.'

They spent the whole afternoon paddling from one island to the next but there was no sign of Qasiagssaq's whale. The men were tired and fed up. They realised he was lying again and decided he should be taught a lesson.

'No more lies,' they shouted. 'You have cheated us for too many years.'

They paddled toward him, encircled his kayak and forced him to paddle to the furthest island they could see. 'We have learned that we will never be able to trust you,' they said. 'The only way you will change is if you learn to survive on your own.'

And with that they took his harpoon and kayak, turned their backs on him and paddled away, leaving him alone to find his own way back home.

Adult-led activities to follow up the story:

▶ Discuss the story – ask the children why they think the village people left Qasiagssaq stranded on the island. Talk about the risks involved with lying. Talk about the benefits of working together and helping each other.

▶ Ask the children to make suggestions for an alternative ending to the story – could the villagers have handled the situation in a different way?

▶ Look at how Inuit people make clothing and shoes from sealskin and compare this with the use of leather in Britain.

▶ Use large cardboard boxes to make kayaks for use in the role-play area.

▶ Experiment with freezing different substances, e.g. cooking oil, water, jelly, slime, undiluted washing up liquid, tinned spaghetti and tomato sauce; Allow the children to feel the substances both before and after freezing and ask them to offer verbal descriptions. Encourage the children to make predictions about what will happen. Observe the substances as they defrost and ask the children to describe and explain what they can see happening and make comparisons.

Independent activities

▶ Small world Arctic scene using large blocks of real ice.

▶ Role-play polar bear den.

▶ Freeze objects in large bowls of coloured water and leave out for children to investigate as they melt.

▶ Magnetic fishing game with literacy or numeracy theme.

Songs, rhymes and poems

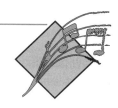

Ice – by Dorothy Aldis.
Find this poem in the Puffin Book of Fantastic First Poems by June Crebbin.

Cold – by Shirley Hughes.
Find this poem in Olly and Me Out and About published by Walker Books.

Polar Bear – by William Jay Smith.
Find this poem on the Internet at:
www.geocities.com/Heartland/1133/animalpoems/polarbears.html.

Links with the EYFS Areas of Learning and Development

PSED – Consider the consequences of their actions for themselves and others; have a positive approach to activities; have an awareness and pride in self; understand what is right, what is wrong, and why.

CLL – Suggest how the story might end; question why things happen and give explanations; use talk to connect ideas, explain what is happening and anticipate what might happen next.

KUW – Show curiosity about how things work; investigate objects and materials by using all of their senses as appropriate; construct with a purpose in mind, using a variety of resources; look closely at similarities, differences and change; ask questions about why things happen.

CD – Work creatively on a large scale.

More stories and information

Ka-ha-si and the Loon: An Eskimo Legend by Terri Cohlene and Charles Reasoner – a young boy is so lazy that no one believes him when he says he can help them out of hunger.

The Polar Bear Son: An Inuit Tale by Lydia Dabcovich – an Inuit woman adopts a baby polar bear that grows up with her and provides her with food.

Arctic Song by Miriam Moss and Adrienne Kennaway – a picture book telling the story of a polar bear and her cubs as they come out of hibernation.

Arctic by DK 24 Hours – an information book detailing a day in the life of a variety of Arctic wildlife with simple text and clear photographs.

Arctic Peoples (Native Americans) by Mir Tamim Ansary – a Heinemann information book for children.

The Partridge and the Fox

France

The little plump partridge noted that there was a slight breeze in the air as she tottered along in the summer sunshine. She was on her way to her favourite perch at the top of the hill where the purple heather was at its thickest. She had spent many an hour up on that hill singing to the rabbits and the bees and especially enjoyed to do so on a day like today.

Little did the partridge know, but she was being watched all the while she wandered up the path by a wily fox hiding in the bushes. In fact, this crafty creature had watched her on many occasions, imagining how tasty and juicy she would be if only he could catch her in his jaws.

The fox was too smart, however, to think that he could simply jump out and grab the partridge without causing her to scream and flap, which would draw the attention of animals from all around. That would not do, after all, hunting is a delicate business and requires stealth, patience and calm.

The little partridge reached the top of the hill and settled herself upon a rock. She took a deep breath and began to sing. Animals and minibeasts emerged from the heather all about and before long there was a great gathering on the path as they danced around to her song.

Meanwhile, the fox lay in the bushes hatching a plan. He knew he would have to outsmart the little partridge and he knew exactly how he was going to do it. Slowly he crept out onto the path and began to dance among the others. One by one, the animals noticed their new companion and fled in fear until it was just the fox and the partridge left. 'Well, well, well, little partridge,' clapped the fox. 'You have the voice of a nightingale!' Although a little alarmed by the appearance of the fox, the partridge was pleased to hear his words of praise and she puffed out her chest in pride.

'However,' the fox added. 'There is something missing – something you are not doing that would make your melody even sweeter.'

'Oh? What's that?' asked the little partridge.

'Did you ever hear your dear mother sing?' asked the fox. 'She had the voice of a warbler! You see, her secret was to close her eyes and completely lose herself in the song.'

'Oh yes? Well, I shall give it a try,' said the partridge and she closed her eyes and began to sing again.

As the fox had promised, she soon became lost in her own song and forgot how dangerous her audience could be. The fox watched her for a while, biding his time and waiting for the right moment to pounce. He listened until she reached her last note and then suddenly made his move. He was as quick as lightening as he leapt in the air and grabbed her between his jaws. The partridge let out a loud squawk but before she could gain the attention of the other animals, the fox had whisked her away down the path.

Before long, they reached a small hump bridge leading into town where an old washerwoman was working down by the river.

'Look!' shouted the washerwoman. 'That fox is running away with the little partridge!'

The fox just grinned and kept on running. Although scared, the partridge was determined to keep her head and knew she had to outsmart the fox.

'Fox!' she shouted. 'You are obviously proud to have caught such a fine bird as me. Why don't you shout back to the washerwoman and tell her how clever you are.'

Although the fox was a clever creature, he was also a boastful one and couldn't resist the temptation to brag about his catch.

'You are right!' he called back to the washerwoman. 'I have caught the little partridge and I am going to take her home for supper whether you like it or not!'

However, to speak, the fox had no choice but to open his mouth. The little partridge grabbed the opportunity to wriggle free. She flapped her wings and flew up to the highest branch of a nearby tree. The fox knew he had blown his only chance. He would never be able to get near the little partridge again.

'Ha. Well farewell, little partridge,' he said. 'You have taught me a good lesson. From now on I will only talk when I have to.'

'Farewell, fox,' replied the partridge. 'You too have taught me a lesson. I will now only close my eyes to sleep!'

Adult-led activities to follow up the story

▶ Circle time – Use the story to introduce a personal safety theme; Explore the question, what should children do when they don't feel safe?

▶ Discuss why the fox has been chosen as a 'bad' character; encourage the children to think about its features – claws, long snout, fast legs and big sharp teeth. Can the children think of any other nasty animal characters from stories (e.g. wolf, alligator, snake, hyena)? Make comparisons.

▶ Ask children to choose an animal that they think would be suitable as a 'bad' character. Provide a range of materials for children to make glove puppets of their characters.

▶ Play a blindfold game that involves the children feeling objects and guessing what they are. A variation of the game might be to ask other children to describe the objects and for the blindfolded child to guess on the basis of verbal clues only.

▶ Set up some practical mathematical activities using fox and partridge picture cards. Pose problems to the children, i.e. share out partridges among foxes, find one more/less partridge, add sets of partridges together, decide which set has more/less partridges/foxes.

Independent activities

▶ Set up a puppet theatre for the children to use their hand-made puppets.

▶ Set up a stage outside with prop microphones for singing performances.

▶ Set up a small world animal farm with foxes and other predators.

▶ Play a matching pairs game featuring birds that are bred or hunted for food, e.g. chickens, ducks, partridges, geese, pheasants, quail.

Songs, rhymes and poems

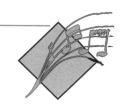

Foxy's creeping around the farm
Find this action rhyme in This Little Puffin.

A Fox Came into my Garden – by Charles Causley.
Find this poem in The Oxford Treasury of Children's Poems.

Frere Jacques
Find this French traditional song with music on the Internet at:
http://bussongs.com/songs/frere_jacques.php.

Links with the EYFS Areas of Learning and Development

PSED – Begin to recognise danger and know who to turn to for help.

CLL – Describe principal characters from stories; show an understanding of the elements of stories, such as main character; use a widening range of words to express or elaborate on ideas; sustain attentive listening.

PSRN – In practical activities and discussion, begin to use the vocabulary involved in adding and subtracting; use language such as 'more' or 'less' to compare two numbers.

KUW – Identify some features of living things; construct with a purpose in mind, using a variety of resources; use simple tools and techniques competently and appropriately.

CD – Create puppets.

More stories and information

The Sly Fox and the Little Red Hen by Vera South – the Ladybird version of the traditional tale featuring a crafty fox.

The Fox and the Crow by Mairi Mackinnon and Rocio Martinez – Aesop's fable about another wily fox.

The Cat Who Walked Across France by Kate Banks and Georg Hallensleben – a cat travels across France to return home.

Fox's Socks by Julia Donaldson and Axel Scheffler – a fox has lost his socks.

France ABCs by Sharon Kaz Cooper and Stacey Previn – an informative book designed especially for young children.

Cat, Dog and Monkey

Indonesia

'Yeaowl!' screeched the cat as it scrabbled about in the dust and tried to keep a grip on a big juicy leg of meat.

Earlier that day, while the cat had been out on her morning stroll, she had come across this tasty find hanging drying in the sun outside a neighbour's hut. It had taken a great deal of effort to get the meat down and the cat had been rather pleased with herself, smiling as she dragged it back towards her home.

Unfortunately for her, a passing dog had caught the scent of the meat and had snuck up and attempted to grab it out of her claws. The cat and the dog had been fighting over the meat for the past two hours and neither was any closer to winning.

'Grrrr, give me the meat!' growled the dog, clamping his jaws tighter around the bone.

'Never in a million years!' meowed the cat, digging her claws in further.

'You know I'll win in the end,' the dog threatened.

'I can hold on for longer than you think,' replied the cat. 'It's my meat anyway. I found it first.'

'You should have got it home sooner then,' barked the dog.

As the afternoon drew on both animals were getting more and more tired and it was becoming clear that neither was going to win very soon.

A cheeky little monkey had been watching everything from up in a nearby banana tree.

'I think I can have some fun here,' he thought and giggling to himself, he swung down to the ground to get closer to the action. 'Why don't you both just share the meat between you?' he called out.

Surprised at the sound of the monkey's voice, both animals lost grip of the meat and dropped it on the ground. They looked up at the monkey, who was standing over them with his hands on his hips, sporting a broad grin from ear to ear.

'I know just the way we can make sure the meat is shared out fairly,' he said, scampering off into the nearby trees.

After a few moments he returned with some pieces of wood, some very large leaves and a couple of vines. Using these materials he built a set of weighing scales and proudly stood them in front of the cat and the dog.

'Now, the fairest way to settle this argument, is to divide the meat in two halves,' the monkey explained. 'These scales are going to help us make sure that each half is the same size so you both get an equal amount.'

The monkey took hold of the meat, tore it in two and placed one piece on each side of the scales. All three animals watched as the scales tilted up and down like a see-saw. When they finally came to a halt one side was resting lower than the other.

'Oops. That side is heavier,' said the monkey, pointing to the lower scale. 'That means the pieces are not equal. I know what, I'll just even it up a bit.'

He took the heavier piece of meat, chewed some off and put it back on the scales. The animals watched again as the scales tipped from one side to the next before balancing themselves. This time, however, they were tilted to the other side.

'Oh dear,' said the monkey. 'Now the other piece of meat is heavier. I'll have to even it up again.'

So the crafty little monkey took up the other piece of meat and took another big chomp.

'Now, don't worry, I think I've got it this time,' he said, putting the meat back on the scales.

The dog and the cat looked at each other and licked their lips as the scales came to a rest yet again.

'Oh no, look at that, I just can't seem to get it right – that side is heavier now,' the monkey said, taking another bite from the meat. By now the portions of meat were getting rather small and despite several more attempts the mischievous little monkey was no closer to balancing the weight.

'I'm so sorry about this,' he said, placing a piece of bone on one side of the scales and the last piece of meat on the other. At last the scales balanced and the cat and the dog leapt up ready to take their share. The monkey was too quick for them however, and grabbed the last piece of meat, tucked it into his mouth and swung back up into the trees.

'Enjoy your bone!' he shouted and disappeared into the forest.

Adult-led activities to follow up the story

▶ Discuss the story – ask the children why they think the monkey was able to trick the cat and dog. Talk about being fair and sharing. Think about situations that require collaboration and consider the consequences of conflict.

▶ Read Cool Cat, Hot Dog by Sandy Turner and study the artwork. Ask the children to choose their favourite breeds of cats and dogs from books. Help them to make split-pin pictures of their chosen animals with moving parts.

▶ Find out about the variety of animals kept as pets in different countries around the world.

▶ Present children with a number of problems involving balancing the weights of different objects and substances using rocker/bucket scales – use things that are easy to increase and decrease, e.g. sand, flour, unifix cubes and marbles, or edible items such as grapes or raisins.

▶ Find out about the plight of the orang-utan – they now only exist on the Indonesian islands of Borneo and Sumatra. Consider the meaning of extinction. Launch an awareness campaign; ask children to make posters.

Independent activities

▶ Play 'I Wanna Be Like You' from the Jungle Book soundtrack in the outdoor area for the children to dance and move like primates.

▶ Provide some metric weights for the children to experiment with independently as an extension of the adult-led weight activity.

▶ Do jigsaw puzzles featuring monkeys, cats or dogs.

▶ Provide art materials for children to make face masks of dogs, cats and monkeys.

Songs, rhymes and poems

Monkey Me – by C J Heck.
Find this poem on the Internet at:
www.authorsden.com/visit/viewPoetry.asp?id=158855.

Ten Little Monkeys – Anon.
Find this counting rhyme in Early Years Poems and Rhymes, published by Scholastic.

Bow Wow Meow Meow: It's Rhyming Cats and Dogs – by Douglas Florian – a compilation of poems about cats and dogs.

Links with the EYFS Areas of Learning and Development

PSED – Take turns and share fairly, understanding that there needs to be agreed values and codes of behaviour for groups of people to work together harmoniously; consider the consequences of their words and actions for themselves and others; show care and concern for living things and the environment.

PSRN – Use language such as 'lesser', 'greater', 'heavier' and 'lighter' to compare quantities.

KUW – Realise tools (hole-punches) can be used for a purpose; use simple tools and techniques competently and appropriately; show an interest in why things happen; Show understanding of cause/effect relations.

PD – Show increasing control in holding and using hole-punches; use increasing control over an object (split-pin).

More stories and information

Monkey Tales by Laurel Dee Gugler and Vlasta Van Kampen – three folktales about monkeys, including Cat, Dog and Monkey.

Monkey and Me by Emily Gravett – a little girl and her monkey pretend to move like all kinds of animals.

The Monkey with a Bright Blue Bottom by Steve Smallman and Nick Schon – a monkey tries to brighten up his appearance.

Monkey Portraits by Jill Greenberg – a quirky book of photographs of apes and monkeys.

Welcome to the World of Orangutans by Diane Swanson – easily accessible information book for young children.

Durrell Wildlife Conservation Trust website – for information, photographs, video footage and factsheets about orang-utans go to
www.durrell.org/Animals/Mammals/Sumatran-orangutan/

The Monkey's Heart

India

The monkey offered his friend the crocodile another juicy mango and the two friends sat on the bank of the River Ganges watching the sun gradually sink into the water.

'Well it's time I must be off dear pal,' **said the crocodile**. 'It's nearly dark and my wife will be wondering where I am.'

He slowly lifted his belly off the ground, dragged himself down the riverbank and slid into the water.

'Well have a lovely evening,' **said the monkey** as he waved his chum off and swung back up into the trees.

When the crocodile got home to his wife, she was indeed wondering where he had been.

'I've been eating mangoes with the monkey on the riverbank,' **the crocodile explained**. 'He sent you some to eat with your dinner,' he added, handing his wife three big ripe pieces of fruit.

'I do not understand your friendship with that monkey,' **said his wife**. 'You are the Ganges most feared predator and yet you lie about with the animal you should be hunting and eat fruit!'

'We have been friends for a long time. I could never hunt the monkey,' **the crocodile replied**.

'Well, I am fed up with eating fish and fruit,' **his wife shouted**. 'It is time you live up to your fearsome reputation and start hunting some meat for me. With all the mangoes that little monkey eats, I bet his heart is as sweet as nectar. I want that heart and I want you to bring it to me!'

'You want me to kill my friend? I cannot possibly do so!' the crocodile cried in dismay.

'Well if you don't, I shall refuse to eat anything else until you change your mind!' The crocodile was in a real fix! He had no choice but to go after his friend and bring him home to his greedy wife. The next evening he swam over to the riverbank to greet the monkey as usual. Today though he planned to lure him out into the water.

'Well hello there dear friend,' he called to the monkey, who was sitting by the water's edge waiting. 'I've been thinking. Each day we sit and eat the mangoes off this tree when there are all kinds of exotic treats we could taste on the other side of the river. Why don't you hop on my back and I will take you across to sample some new delights.'

The monkey had no reason not to trust the crocodile and so accepted his offer. With thoughts of rose-apples and jack-fruit, he jumped onto his friend's back and they headed out onto the river. When they got about half way across the crocodile suddenly ducked under the water, sending the monkey floundering about for something to keep him afloat.

'What are you doing?' cried the monkey. 'You know I cannot swim!'

'I'm very sorry monkey,' said the crocodile, 'but I can no longer be friends with you. I am taking you home to my wife so she can eat your heart for her dinner.'

Although the monkey was surprised at this sudden betrayal, he knew there was no time to worry. He was cleverer than the crocodile and needed a story that would help him get away as quick as possible.

'Well, that is a shame,' he said. 'I don't have my heart with me today.'

'What are you talking about?' exclaimed the crocodile.

'Didn't you know?' said the monkey. 'Monkeys don't wear their hearts all the time otherwise they would be battered about while we swing in the trees. No, we take our hearts out before we start jumping around. Look, you can see all our hearts hanging over there,' he added, pointing to a nearby bunch of fig trees.

The crocodile was surprised at this, but believed the monkey anyway.

'Well then, you must take me to your heart, so I can take it back to my wife,' he said.

'I don't see that I have any choice,' said the monkey. 'If I stay out here I will drown.'

The crocodile allowed the monkey to crawl back onto his back and set off in the direction of the fig trees. When they arrived the monkey pointed out the fattest fig in the nearest tree.

'That, my friend, is my heart. If you will allow me to, I will climb up there and fetch it down for you.'

The crocodile obliged and the monkey sprang up into the tree. He grabbed the fig and threw it down to the crocodile.

'Now take that nice big juicy fig back to your wife and tell her I hope she enjoys it!' he laughed and disappeared into the trees.

The crocodile's wife never did forgive him and neither did the monkey.

Adult-led activities to follow up the story

▶ Discuss the story – ask the children how they feel about the crocodile and how he treated his friend the monkey. Talk about friendship and betrayal.

▶ Find out about the difference between crocodiles and alligators.

▶ Use the book River Story by Meredith Hooper and Bee Willey to learn about rivers – looking at their origins and journey to sea. Find out the difference between rivers, lakes, streams and canals.

▶ Visit a river – take care to carry out a thorough risk assessment beforehand.

▶ Make floating crocodiles by painting plastic bottles. Waterproof them with PVA glue and be sure to retain lids. Float them down the river system (see independent activities below).

▶ Talk about how people and animals cannot survive without a heart. Find out about the importance of having a healthy heart and how to keep it healthy. Undertake different levels of physical activity and encourage children to monitor their heart rates.

Independent activities

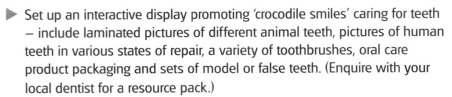

▶ Create a slime swamp for small world play with crocodiles.

▶ Provide a range of water trays and pieces of guttering for the children to create river systems outside.

▶ Set up an interactive display promoting 'crocodile smiles' caring for teeth – include laminated pictures of different animal teeth, pictures of human teeth in various states of repair, a variety of toothbrushes, oral care product packaging and sets of model or false teeth. (Enquire with your local dentist for a resource pack.)

Songs, rhymes and poems

Crocodile – Anon.
Find this poem in Elephants and Emus and Other Animal Rhymes by Philippa-Alys Browne.

The Crocodile – by Roald Dahl.
Find this rhyme in Dirty Beasts, published by Puffin.

Down the River
Find this song on the Internet at **www.singup.org**.

Links with the EYFS Areas of Learning and Development

PSED – Can be caring towards each other; form good relationships with adults and peers; Show confidence and the ability to stand up for their own rights.

KUW – Find out about and identify some features of living things; observe, find out about and identify features in the place they live and the natural world; show curiosity about why empty plastic bottles float and how they might travel on water.

PD – Observe the effects of activity on their bodies; show some understanding that good practices with regard to exercise can contribute to good health; recognise the changes that happen to their bodies when they are active.

More stories and information

I Really Want to Eat a Child by Sylvianne Donnio and Dorothee Monfried – a baby crocodile is fed up with bananas and fancies something different to eat.

Siddharth and Rinki by Addy Farmer and Karin Littlewood – tells the tale of a little Indian boy who has come to live in Britain.

Elephant Dance: A Journey Through India by Theresa Heine and Sheila Moxley – a book about the importance of the elephant in Indian culture.

The Gingerbread Man by Estelle Corke – in this traditional tale the predator wins.

Stories from the Panchatantra – for many more stories go to
www.indianhindunames.com/panchatantra-stories.htm

Wake Up Shake Up Productions website – a programme for promoting short bursts of exercise throughout the school day. For more information go to
www.wakeupshakeup.com

The Lion and the Nien

China

Long ago the Chinese lived in constant fear of being terrorised by a fierce and angry creature that stalked into villages to hunt and eat people. This terrifying creature, known as the Nien, had fiery red eyes, horns and razor sharp teeth and was not afraid of anything.

The people of one village had sent a fox after it, only to watch as it was gobbled up. They then sent a tiger, which the Nien chased away with its tail between its legs. The villagers knew that at any moment the Nien might charge into the village and grab a child for its dinner! Everyone was so afraid to come out of their houses that they had hardly made any preparations for the fast approaching New Year festival.

The villagers knew they had to do something; after all they couldn't stay indoors forever. They had heard about the fierce reputation of the mighty lion and thought that perhaps he might succeed where the others had not. The lion was pleased to help the villagers. He had heard the awful stories about the Nien and thought it was time it was taught a lesson.

After a few days, the Nien came creeping back into the village. The lion hid patiently in the shadows and watched as the Nien crept through gardens and peered in windows, looking for an easy meal. As it got closer the lion gradually crouched himself into pouncing position and fixed a tooth-baring grimace upon his face. When the Nien was close enough he leapt out with a deafening roar. The startled Nien stumbled backwards and fell over its back legs.

As it writhed around on the ground the lion jumped forwards and locked his jaws around its neck. The Nien let out a bloodcurdling cry, struggled free and fled from the village as fast as it could. The villagers came rushing outside clapping and cheering.

'We are free! Three cheers for the lion!'

'We are free! Three cheers for the lion!'

They celebrated by throwing a big party for the lion to show him how grateful they were.

As the New Year approached excitement grew amongst the villagers. They busied themselves cleaning and decorating their houses and strung up lanterns in the streets. Then the day before the celebrations were due to begin, a little boy came running into the village screaming. 'Run! Hide! The Nien is back and it looks very angry!'

The villagers ran straight to the lion.

'I'm so sorry my friends,' said the lion. 'I cannot come and help until after the New Year. I have been commanded by the emperor to guard the palace gates.'

The villagers were distraught.

'The Nien is not scared of anything except the lion. What are we going to do?' they asked.

'If the Nien is only frightened of the lion, then it is the lion that we must use to scare it away,' replied one man.

He explained his plan and everyone began to murmur and whisper amongst themselves in excitement. They rushed back to their houses and collected all kinds of materials; red, yellow and orange coloured paper and paint, glue and pieces of cane. They worked together long into the night.

The next day, they played loud music in the streets to fool the Nien into thinking the festivities were beginning. They lit the lanterns, locked their children indoors and lay in wait. Sure enough the music soon lured the Nien into the village. The villagers watched as it skulked down the main street, snout to the ground sniffing for children. The villagers held their breath, waiting for it to draw near. As it came closer, they whispered a countdown; three, two, one... charge!

The Nien froze as a lion as big as a dragon leapt out from the shadows, bearing enormous teeth and shaking a huge bulky mane. Its roar sounded as tremendous as a hundred voices. The lion bounded toward the Nien and encircled it, jumping from side to side. It seemed to be dancing. As it got closer and closer the Nien began to panic. Knowing it was no match for such a magnificent creature, it turned and ran away as fast as it could.

'Hooray!' cheered the villagers as they climbed out from under the lion costume.

'We are finally free of the Nien!'

The children came running outside and everyone partied throughout the rest of the day and into the night.

Now every year people all over China dress up in magnificent lion costumes and celebrate the coming of the New Year with a lion dance. The Nien has never bothered anyone again.

Adult-led activities to follow up the story

▶ Find out about Chinese New Year customs. Ask the children to think about festivals that they and their families celebrate. Talk about and compare.

▶ Make lion dance costumes: Dress everyone up in red and yellow clothes and paint their faces; create and decorate enormous lion masks to be held up at the front; then arrange children into groups of five to create each lion (one child to hold head and others to link up one behind the other as the lion's body).

▶ Watch a video of a traditional lion dance. Using a large space, play some Chinese New Year music and allow the children to make up their own lion dances using their costumes.

▶ Explain the concept of fortune cookies. Encourage the children to write a message of good fortune.

▶ Look at some pictures of the Great Wall of China. Challenge the children to build their own great wall using large wooden construction blocks. Extend the task by challenging the children to ensure that it is strong enough to stand on safely.

Independent activities

▶ Challenge the children to paint pictures of what they believe the Nien might look like.

▶ Provide a range of materials, e.g. straws, lolly sticks, tissue paper, glue, sugar paper, card, wiggly eyes, for children to make dancing dragons.

▶ Role-play a Chinese take-away.

▶ Boil egg and rice noodles in food colouring, drizzle with oil and leave out for children to investigate.

Songs, rhymes and poems

I'm a lion in the forest and I'm looking for my tea – Barbara Ireson.
Find this poem in This Little Puffin published by Puffin Books.

The Lion – by Hilaire Belloc.
Find this poem in The Bad Child's Book of Beasts published by Red Fox.

Lion Dance Song
Find this song with a selection of others about Chinese New Year on the Internet at **www.canteach.ca/elementary/songspoems54.html**

Links with the EYFS Areas of Learning and Development

PSED – Talk freely about their home and community; make choices that involve challenge when adults ensure their safety.

CLL – Speak clearly and audibly with confidence and control and show awareness of the listener; use their phonic knowledge to write simple regular words and make phonetically plausible attempts at more complex words.

KUW – Recognise some special times in their lives and the lives of others; gain an awareness of the cultures and beliefs of others; join construction pieces together to build and balance.

CD – Work creatively on a large scale (to create a lion head mask); imitate and create movement in response to music; begin to move rhythmically.

More stories and information

Lion Dancer: Ernie Wan's Chinese New Year by Kate Waters, Madeline Slovenz-Low and Martha Cooper – the festival through the eyes of a young boy with photos instead of illustrations.

Lanterns and Firecrackers: A Chinese New Year Story by Jonny Zucker and Jan Barger Cohen – a simple explanation of customs and festivities.

Dragon Dance by Joan Holub and Benrei Huang – a lift the flap book.

Watching Lions in Africa by Richard Spilsbury and Louise Spilsbury – simple layout with a lot of detail (useful to explain where lions really come from).

Yum Yum Dim Sum by Amy Wilson Sanger – a simple introduction to Chinese food with interesting collaged pictures.

The Monster Bed by Jeanne Willis and Suzanne Varley – a lovely story about a little monster that is scared of finding humans under his bed.

Anansi and the Box of Stories

Ghana, Africa

Anansi the spider loved stories. However, he and his family had to tell the same ones over and over again because they did not know many. It was very rare that they had the opportunity to hear a new tale because there were so very few in the world. Nyame the Sky God kept them all locked in a wooden trunk and refused to share them.

One evening after listening to the same old yarns, Anansi decided it was time Nyame shared out some of his stories. So he threw a line of thread up into the clouds and climbed up to see him.

'Nyame, it is unfair that you keep all the stories of the world locked up. I plead with you to give them out and allow everyone to share in their enjoyment.'

'You cannot expect me to give you such precious treasure for free,' laughed Nyame. 'I will consider giving you the stories for a price. Bring me Onini the python, Osebo the leopard, Mmboro the hornets and Mmoatia the spirit.'

'Mmoatia!' exclaimed Anansi. 'I can never hope to catch an invisible spirit.'

'That is the price. Bring me all four or you will never hear a new story again.'

Anansi thought hard to make a plan. Deciding to start with Onini the python, he grabbed a piece of bamboo and wandered into the jungle muttering to himself.

'They are all wrong. There is no way this cane is as long as the great Onini.'

Just as Anansi planned, Onini was writhing around the branches above listening. He swung his head down out of the trees and the two were suddenly nose-to-nose.

'What isss thisss that I hear you dissscusssing with yoursssself?' he asked.

'Oh hello there Onini. Perhaps you can help me. I think this cane has got to be shorter than you, but everyone else disagrees.'

Onini couldn't pass up an opportunity to show off.

48

'Why don't I ssstretch myssself out and you can measure me againssst the cane.'

Anansi laid the cane on the ground and Onini slithered alongside it. Without hesitation, he sprung on top of the snake and spun a web binding him to the cane.

He proudly took him to Nyame. 'Very clever,' said Nyame, 'but you still have three more to capture.'

Carrying a large sack with him, Anansi ventured back into the jungle, found a clearing and sat on a rock.

'My wife is so wrong,' he said loudly. 'There is no way the mighty leopard Osebo would fit into a sack as small as this.'

Just as Anansi planned, Osebo curiously stalked out from amongst the trees.

'You are right about one thing,' Osebo growled, 'I am the mightiest of all the animals.'

'You truly are,' replied Anansi. 'That is why I believe there is no way you would ever fit in a sack as small as this.'

'We shall prove your wife wrong then,' Osebo said and he climbed into the sack.

Anansi quickly tied the top, slung the leopard over his shoulder and carried him to Nyame.

Anansi soaked himself in water before visiting Mmboro the hornets. Taking with him more water and an empty gourd shell, he climbed the tree from which their nest was hanging and poured some water in the top. The Mmboro flew out in fury.

'What's going on?' they buzzed angrily.

'We just had the heaviest rain shower,' Anansi lied. 'Here, would you like to shelter in my gourd shell while your nest dries out?'

The hornets thanked Anansi and flew into the gourd. Anansi hastily spun a web over the hole, trapping them inside and took them to Nyame.

'You are very cunning, but let's see if you can catch Mmoatia,' Nyame taunted.

This was the challenge that Anansi dreaded the most. As well as being invisible, Mmoatia was an evil spirit who could kill with just her touch. He needed something to distract her. He carved a doll out of wood, covered it in sticky sap from a gum tree and stood it up. He then hid in some nearby bushes and waited. After a while Anansi was startled by a loud voice.

'Why won't you speak?' shouted Mmoatia.

Of course the doll could not speak. Anansi saw it suddenly nudge to one side. Mmoatia was angry and trying to kill it.

'Aaarrgh!' she shrieked. 'Let me go!'

Anansi could not see Mmoatia but knew her hand was stuck to the doll. He watched it move again as she let out another scream. She had both hands stuck now. Anansi scurried out from the bushes and spun a web around the spirit, tying her to the doll.

Nyame was furious. He had no choice but to give Anansi the chest. Proud Anansi took it down to earth and eagerly opened it, releasing thousands of stories that flew all over the world for all to share and enjoy forever more.

Adult-led activities to follow up the story

▶ Discuss the story – ask the children what they think about Nyame's plan to keep hold of all the stories. Talk about kindness and sharing. Ask the children what it would be like to live in a world without stories.

▶ Home task – ask parents to write or record their child's favourite story that they like to be told orally. Collect the stories in a box and share them with the rest of the class/group.

▶ Invite parents in to share their stories with the class.

▶ Read a range of Anansi stories. Make up a story about Anansi together as a class. Ask the children to think of their own Anansi stories and make mini storybooks.

▶ Carry out a class survey asking the children which is their favourite genre of story, e.g. fairytale, action adventure, multicultural, true stories or animal stories. Make a bar chart or pictogram using a computer program such as 2Simple to show the results. Allow the children to survey each other using tally charts.

▶ Find out about exotic spiders. Use straws/doweling and string/silver wool to make spider webs.

Independent activities

▶ Provide a range of materials, e.g. straws, lolly sticks, tissue paper, glue, egg boxes, card, wiggly eyes, pipe-cleaners, string, wool, for children to make spiders and webs.

▶ Set up a vivarium containing spiders for the children to observe web spinning. Provide minibeast collection equipment for the children to hunt and collect spiders.

▶ Make some blank mini books and put them out with drawing and writing materials for the children to use to make little storybooks.

▶ Make snakes with playdough; provide rulers for measuring the length.

▶ Experiment with measuring worms (available from **www.tts-group.co.uk**).

Songs, rhymes and poems

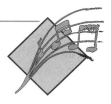

Incy Wincy Spider
Find this rhyme and others on a CD of the same name published by BBC Audiobooks Ltd.

Kye Kye Kule – by the Fanti Tribe, Ghana.
Find this nonsense action rhyme in Skip Across the Ocean published by Frances Lincoln.

There's a Spider on the Floor
Find this song on the Internet at **www.singup.org**.

Links with the EYFS Areas of Learning and Development

CLL – Have some favourite stories; listen with enjoyment, respond to and make up their own stories; begin to be aware of the way stories are structured; show an understanding of the elements of stories; attempt writing for different purposes, using features of different forms, such as stories; use their phonic knowledge to write simple regular words and make phonetically plausible attempts at more complex words; use a pencil and hold it effectively to form recognisable letters.

PSRN – Begin to represent numbers using marks on paper; learn to classify and organise; begin to make comparisons between quantities.

KUW – Complete a simple program on the computer to create a pictogram.

PD – Engage in activities requiring hand-eye coordination.

More stories and information

Anansi and the Box of Stories: A West African Folktale by Stephen Krensky and Jeni Reeves – an illustrated version of the featured story.

Anansi does the Impossible! by Verna Aardema and Lisa Desimini – a shorter version.

Anancy and the Sky God by Ladybird Books – another account.

Clever Anansi and the Boastful Bullfrog by 'H' Patten and John Clementson – Anansi teaches the noisy bullfrog a lesson.

The Illustrated Anansi by Philip M. Sherlock and Petrina Wright – a compilation of four Anansi stories.

National Film Board of Canada: Focus on Animation website – for a good quality animated Anansi tale go to:
www3.nfb.ca/animation/objanim/en/films/film.php?sort=cc&id=50422

The Rat's Wedding

Pakistan

One morning a little rat was digging around at the foot of a tree looking for some fallen fruit for his breakfast when he came across a loose dry root. Knowing how useful such finds can be, he tucked it under his arm and set off back home. Along his way he passed a man crouched at the side of the road frantically trying to light a fire while his two children cried and wailed at his side.

'What on earth is the matter?' asked the rat.

'My children are desperately hungry and I cannot cook for them without a fire,' replied the man. 'This wood is too damp to get a spark from.'

'Well, why don't you have this big dry root I found?' offered the rat. 'It is sure to get your fire started.'

The man was very grateful and thanked him by giving him some bread dough to eat. Pleased with himself for doing such a good deed, the rat skipped off down the road. Before long, he came across two little boys stood outside the front door of their house, crying.

'Whatever could be the matter?' asked the rat.

'Our parents are still at work and we cannot get indoors,' the boys explained. 'It is now getting late and we are hungry for our dinner.'

'Well, why don't you eat this bread dough?' offered the rat.

The little boys were so relieved that they thanked him by giving him a clay pot. The rat trotted off again, pleased with himself for being so kind. Further down the road he came across a man milking a buffalo. He noticed that the man did not have a bucket, but instead was using a dirty old boot to collect the milk!

'Why, you cannot use a dirty old boot to collect milk with!' cried the rat. 'Here, use this clay pot, it is much cleaner.'

The man was so grateful that he offered the rat some milk in return. By now the little rat was starting to think an awful lot of himself and was beginning to believe that others should think the same way. 'Is that all you are going to offer me?' he asked in the most ungrateful way.

'Without my help you would be drinking your milk from a smelly old boot. I think I deserve more. Give me your buffalo!'

The man was so surprised at the rat's bravado that he laughed and tied the buffalo's rope around his neck. Before the rat knew what was happening the buffalo charged off in search of some grass to graze on, dragging the rat behind him. This continued all afternoon until the buffalo finally stopped to drink at a stream. As it lazily slurped at the water a wedding procession passed by. At the tail of the procession four men were carrying the bride in a curtained carriage. All four looked terribly unhappy.

'Why do you hold such grumpy faces on a day as joyous as this?' asked the rat.

'We have been carrying this carriage for miles and have had nothing to eat all the way.'

'Take this buffalo,' said the rat. 'It will be scrumptious to eat roasted.'

The men were so happy that they offered the rat some meat. But he was far from grateful for this offer and puffed out his chest in disgust.

'I give you a whole buffalo to cure your hunger and you offer me a measly piece of meat! That is simply not good enough. I think I deserve a new bride!'

The four men were so surprised by the rat's boldness that they ran away scared, leaving the carriage behind. The rat couldn't believe his luck when he peered inside to see the most beautiful princess he had ever seen. He grabbed her hand and took her home. By now it was time for dinner. The rat fetched two peas and put them in the palm of the princess' hand.

'Two peas are not going to satisfy my hunger!' she cried. 'I need rice and cakes and sweet eggs to fill me up.'

'Well then, tomorrow I shall give you a basket of plums to sell at the market. You can use the money to buy food to your taste,' replied the rat.

The next morning the princess went to the market, closely followed by the rat. There, she was spotted by the king's guards, who picked her up and took her back to the castle. The rat was furious at losing his bride. He ran up to the castle door and beat it with his little fists. The queen opened the door and smiled at him.

'I want my bride!' the rat demanded.

'Of course you do,' said the queen. 'Come inside, we have prepared a cosy warm room for you.'

The rat followed the queen inside and through to the kitchen. There, the queen opened a stove door and without thinking, the rat jumped straight inside and the queen shut the door. Quickly realising his mistake, he pleaded with her.

'I have learned my lesson. No more bargains. Please let me out!'

Lucky for him, the queen did let the rat out and he never made a bargain again.

Adult-led activities to follow up the story

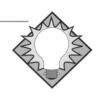

▶ Discuss the story – ask the children what they think of the rat. Look back at how the story started with the rat simply being helpful and kind. Consider where it went wrong for the rat. Talk about the consequences of being greedy.

▶ Research pet rats with the children. Allow the group to choose a type of rat that can be cared for as a pet in the setting. Involve the children in setting up a suitable enclosure. Ensure they share in care-taking responsibilities, such as feeding and cleaning.

▶ Invite a speaker from your local council's waste management department in to talk about responsible rubbish disposal and problems with wild rats.

▶ Make rats using clay.

▶ Find out about the Water Buffalo that is native to Asia and kept as a domestic farm animal. Melt some Buffalo mozzarella cheese and taste it.

▶ Bake bread.

▶ Challenge the children to make mini rat-runs using junk. Test the runs by dragging through rats made with stuffed socks. Ask the children to evaluate their work and adapt it where needed.

Independent activities

▶ Create a rat run outside; set out an obstacle course that entails crawling in, through, under and over.

▶ Make slime using soap flakes. Cut up some plastic washing line to make rats' tails and mix into the slime for children to look for and 'catch'.

▶ Role-play a rat hole.

▶ Play 'Pin the Tail on the Rat'.

▶ Provide a programmable toy such as BeeBot and an alphabet mat for children to spell out as many words as they can think of rhyming with rat.

▶ Play matching games with cvc word and picture cards.

Songs, rhymes and poems

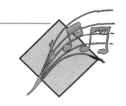

'He was a rat' – by Anon
Find this poem in The New Faber Book of Children's Poems.

To market – by Anon
Find this rhyme in Early Years Poems and Rhymes published by Scholastic.

Curry and rice – by Elizabeth Bennett
Find this song in This Little Puffin published by Puffin Books.

Links with the EYFS Areas of Learning and Development

PSED – Show care and concern for living things; be confident to try new things; express likes/dislikes; appreciate the need for hygiene.

KUW – Show curiosity and interest in the features of living things; show an awareness of change (melting mozzarella and baking dough); are interested in pushing and pulling things; build and construct with a wide range of objects, selecting appropriate resources and adapting their work where necessary.

PD – Explore malleable materials by patting, stroking, squeezing, pinching and twisting them.

CD – Create clay models.

More stories and information

Pakistani Folk Tales: Toontoony Pie and Other Stories by Ashraf Siddiqui and Marilyn Lerch – contains a version of the featured story.

The Crafty Jackal and Other Stories: Folktales of Punjab by Neera Jain – a collection of stories for young children.

P is for Pakistan by Shazia Razzak and Prodeepta Das – a very simple information book with good quality photographs.

The Five Fingered Family by Siri-Kartar K. Khalsa and Shakta Kaur Khalsa – an illustrated traditional Punjab tale.

Cbeebies website – for an animated story from Pakistan with English and Urdu script called The Painted Jackal go to
www.bbc.co.uk/cbeebies/stories/world/painted_jackal.shtml

The Dragon of Krakow

Poland

'I'm not sure I want to go inside,' said one little boy as he peered into the gloomy darkness.

'Don't be daft. I doubt there's a dragon in there and even if there is we could out-run it easily,' said the eldest boy.

Feeling frightened and excited all at the same time, five little Polish boys began to creep inside the cave of Wawel Hill. They had been told stories of a magnificent fire-breathing dragon that dwelled within and, despite warnings to stay away, they had decided to find out if it was true.

As the boys ventured deeper into the cavern the blackness seemed to close in all around them. Water dripped from the ceiling and the damp air made them shiver.

'I don't think I want to go any further,' murmured the smallest of the boys.

'Don't worry, we'll look after you,' said another and he took his friend's hand.

On they crept, feeling their way along the cave wall, watching out for puddles and bats. The mouth of the cave was getting further and further away and the darkness was getting thicker and thicker.

'Shhhh, I think I can hear something,' whispered the eldest boy.

All five stopped and strained to listen. Sure enough there was a curious sound coming from up ahead.

'It sounds like snoring.'

'I don't like it,' said the smallest boy. 'I want to go home now.' He pulled at his friend's hand. 'Stop fidgeting,' said his friend, giving the little boy a tug.

The little boy lost his footing on the damp rock and let out a small cry as he scrambled to stay upright.

'Shhhh!'

It was too late. The snoring had stopped. All five little boys froze in terror as they stared into the shadows up ahead. Suddenly the cave lit up in a fiery glow of orange and yellow flame. Screaming the boys turned and ran as fast as their legs would carry them, out of the cave, down the hill and back to the village. The dragon was awake!

From that day onwards the villagers lived in constant terror. After many centuries asleep the dragon was as hungry as ever, constantly swooping down from the hill to grab people at random. Many courageous men attempted to slay the beast but were unable to pierce its tough scaly armour with their small arrows and swords. Knowing that they could not hope to kill the dragon alone, the villagers sent word to a wise man called Krakus, who was known for mixing magical potions.

Krakus instructed the villagers to send him a sheep and he set to work mixing a deadly concoction. He covered the sheep in a poisonous mixture and carried it up Wawel Hill. Standing at the mouth of the cave, he shouted, 'Here, chomp on this!' and tossed the sheep inside. Unsuspecting, the dragon gobbled up the sheep with a single gulp.

Meanwhile the villagers waited at the bottom of the hill and watched the mouth of the cave. They had seen Krakus climb back down and were wondering how he had escaped the dragon so quickly.

'Roooarrhhh!'

All of a sudden the earth began to shake as rocks and boulders came rolling down the hillside. The dragon emerged from the cave, holding its stomach and stumbling from side to side. Its belly was burning with Krakus' awful poison.

'Roooarraaaahhh!'

It teetered at the edge for a moment before spreading its wings and lunging forward into the air. The villagers watched in awe as the dragon dove into the valley frantically looking for water. Unable to quench its thirst it drank and drank until its belly began to swell up as round as a balloon. As it drank more, its stomach grew bigger still until all of a sudden there was a massive explosion and its belly burst. The dragon was dead.

'Hooray! We are free,' the villagers rejoiced. 'Krakus you are our hero!'

They built Krakus a grand castle and invited him to be their ruler. Under his command it soon became a thriving city, which the villagers named Krakow in his honour.

Adult-led activities to follow up the story

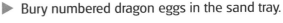

▶ Discuss the story – ask the children to consider what happened when the five little boys went sneaking into the cave. Take photographs of puppets in precarious situations to set up discussion scenarios about the consequences of venturing into dangerous places, e.g. stuck under some timber on a building site, trapped under the wheel of a car in a garage, picking up broken glass.

▶ Experiment with filling balloons with water until they burst.

▶ Make up dragon poems. (See The Little Book of Making Poetry by Keri Finlayson for help and inspiration.)

▶ Make dragons with wings that flap (for a simple method see the video demonstration 'How to make flapping bat wings' on the Internet at **www.ehow.com/video_2369943_make-flapping-bat-wings-halloween.html**).

▶ Visit some caves. (Take care to ensure that the caves are visitor friendly and preferably have organised tours available.)

Independent activities

▶ Set up a small world castle with knights and dragons.

▶ Provide resources for children to build a cave, e.g. clothes horse, blanket, pegs, large wooden blocks, large cardboard boxes.

▶ Role-play a cave with dragon costumes or masks and knight uniforms.

▶ Bury numbered dragon eggs in the sand tray.

▶ Provide red and yellow paint with trays for mixing and creating different fiery colours to make fire paintings.

Songs, rhymes and poems

Dragon – by Olive Dove
Find this poem in the Oxford Treasury of Children's Poems.

Lizzie
Find this Polish lullaby in Skip Across the Ocean published by Frances Lincoln.

Davy Dolldrum dream'd he drove a dragon
Find this tongue twister in Michael Foreman's Nursery Rhymes published by Walker Books.

Links with the EYFS Areas of Learning and Development

PSED – Begin to recognise danger and know who to turn to for help; have an awareness of boundaries set; consider the consequences of their words and actions for themselves and others.

CLL – Make up their own poems; extend their vocabulary, exploring the meanings and sounds of new words; show an awareness of rhyme and alliteration; use their phonic knowledge to write simple regular words and make phonetically plausible attempts at more complex words.

KUW – Describe and talk about what they see; show curiosity about why things happen and how things work; begin to try out a range of tools and techniques safely; observe, find out about and identify features in the natural world.

More stories and information

King Krakus and the Dragon by Janina Domanska – a picture book version of the story.

The Dragon of Krakow and other Polish Stories by Richard Monte and Paul Hess – a collection of stories for children.

Puff the Magic Dragon by Peter Yarrow, Lenny Lipton and Eric Puybaret – the well-known song presented in a picture book with CD.

The Great Dragon Rescue by Mark Robertson – one of a series of books featuring little boy George, protector of dragons.

The Trouble with Dragons by Debi Gliori – a picture book about environmental issues with a twist.

P is for Poland by Agnieska Mrowczynska – a clear and simple information book with good quality photographs.

Teachers TV website – find an animated Polish tale called The Flower of Fern on the Internet at **www.teachers.tv/video/34284**

The Spell-bound Giant

Portugal

Resting her head in her hands, the old woman stared down at two gold coins sitting on the kitchen table.

'How can we possibly live on this?' she asked her two sons.

'Don't worry mother,' said the eldest. 'I will go and find some work to help support the family.'

He packed his bags and set off the next morning. He travelled for days and days through town after town with no prospect of finding work before finally arriving in a small village where he decided to try his luck at a local farm.

'There's nothing here lad,' said the farmer, 'but I have heard that the magician is looking for an assistant.'

The magician was a curious looking man with long white wispy hair and a wart on his nose. He greeted the young man with a bow and said he would employ him for one coin a day if he would agree to travel with him wherever he might go.

The very next morning the young man awoke to find the magician had saddled two horses and packed for a long journey. They travelled non-stop all day and throughout the next night before finally arriving at the foot of a mountain.

'Right then lad,' said the magician. 'My bones are far to frail and old to risk rattling them about on such a steep climb. You are going to ride to the top of that mountain instead.'

'Woooaah!' the young man screamed as the magician flicked his wand to send his horse galloping up to the top of the mountain.

The young man couldn't believe his eyes. All around him there were precious items made of gold, silver and jewels. But strangely, also mixed amongst these treasures were many bones.

'Empty your horse's saddlebags and fill them up with as much treasure as you can,' commanded the magician.

'Yes sir,' the young man said and he set to work.

As soon as he had finished the magician flicked his wand again and summonsed the horse back down the mountain. Then with another flick he knocked the young man off his feet, before turning and galloping away, leaving him stranded at the top.

The young man was devastated. He had been a fool. It was a long way back down the mountain and looking around at the bones on the ground, he knew he must find food. He began to gather some wild herbs. It was then that he made an astonishing discovery. Under the roots of a particularly thick bush of thyme was a huge iron ring, which he noticed was attached to a large wooden trap door. Heaving with all his might, he pulled it open to reveal some stone steps leading down inside the mountain. Curious, the young man crept inside.

He was greeted by the sight of an enormous dinner table set with oversize plates and bowls. Raising his eyes to look all around, he discovered he was in the dining hall of a magnificent palace. There were several closed doors in the surrounding walls. He wandered over to the closest door and opened it to reveal a long narrow hallway. Halfway down this hallway he found another door that was standing slightly ajar.

'Who brought you here?'

The young man stumbled backwards in fright.

'I... I... I found the door,' he mumbled and fell against the wall, knocking himself out.

He awoke to find himself lying on an enormous bed. Hovering over him was the biggest, saddest face he had ever seen.

'How did you find me?'

The young man sat himself up. In front of him stood a very unhappy looking giant. He explained what had happened with the magician and listened as the giant told him how the same magician had cast a spell on his castle, burying it in the mountain.

'I have been trapped in here for over one hundred years and all the while the magician has been stealing my treasure,' the giant said. 'The only way to break the spell is to kill the magician.'

Meanwhile, unbeknown to the young man, his brother had been out searching for him. He had followed much the same path, ending up in the company of the magician and was now outside standing at the top of the mountain. Being suspicious of the magician however, his brother did not fill the saddlebags with treasure, but instead filled them with bones. He then picked up an especially large bone and flung it at the magician's knees, breaking both his legs and sending him falling to the ground. At that moment, the mountain started to shake and the castle began to rise out of the ground.

Inside the castle, the giant rejoiced. 'The spell is broken, but how?'

He and the young man ran outside to find the brother standing there staring with a look of astonishment.

'I am undone!' shouted a voice from the bottom of the mountain.

They ran to the edge and looked down just in time to see the magician disappear. The spell was broken and the giant was a prisoner no more.

Adult-led activities to follow up the story:

▶ While the children are absent, turn over some furniture, tip up some resource boxes and stamp a trail of giant footprints through the setting. Ask the children for suggestions as to what might have happened. Use the incident as a springboard for literacy activities, e.g. composing stories about what might have happened or imagining what the giant's appearance/personality is like.

▶ Assist the children in making a miniature town. Use playground chalk to draw roads, fields, car parks, etc. on the ground outside and create small buildings using painted cardboard boxes. Wander around the town pretending to be giants.

▶ Find out about giant creatures, e.g. giant African land snails, Galápagos giant tortoises, giant squids, giant millipedes.

▶ Teach the children some magic tricks.

▶ Ask the children to draw around each other's body outlines using black sugar paper and chalk. Find out who is the tallest in the class by lining up and arranging the outlines by height. Record results on a height chart.

Independent activities

▶ Turn the climbing frame outside into a castle.

▶ Set up a stage in the outdoor area with magician outfits for magic shows.

▶ Play size sorting activities, e.g. compare bears.

▶ Provide measuring tapes for children to experiment with measuring each other's heights.

Songs, rhymes and poems

Fee Fi Fo Fum
Find a musical activity for this rhyme in Music Express Foundation Stage published by A&C Black.

If you should meet a giant
Find this rhyme in This Little Puffin published by Puffin Books.

Giant's Breakfast by Judith Nicholls
Find this counting rhyme in Early Years Poems and Rhymes published by Scholastic.

Links with the EYFS Areas of Learning and Development

CLL – Consistently develop a simple story, explanation or line of questioning; are intrigued by novelty and events around them; use their phonic knowledge to write simple regular words and make phonetically plausible attempts at more complex words; attempt writing for different purposes.

PSRN – Use language such as 'taller' and 'tallest' to describe size; order two or three items by height.

KUW – Show curiosity and interest in living things.

CD – Express and communicate their ideas and thoughts; use their imagination in imaginative and role-play and stories.

More stories and information

The Smartest Giant in Town by Julia Donaldson and Axel Scheffler – the classic story about a giant who wants to be a little less scruffy.

The Selfish Giant by Oscar Wilde and Michael Foreman – a giant builds a wall around his garden to keep children out.

Daisy and the Trouble with Giants by Kes Gray, Nick Sharratt and Garry Parsons – a little girl wishes she could meet a giant.

My Very Own Lighthouse by Francisco Cunha, translated by Joao Leal – a Portuguese story from the Contemporary Picture Books from Europe series. A little girl is worried about being separated from her father.

In Search of the Hidden Giant by Jeanne Willis and Ruth Brown – lyrical text and opportunities for the children to spot the hidden giants.

Baboushka

Russia

Baboushka was a little old Russian woman, who lived all alone in a large house deep in the forest. She had no family and very few friends. It was very rare that Baboushka ever had visitors and so she kept herself busy by cleaning. Her house was so big that she was forever occupied washing and dusting and polishing and mopping.

One cold winter night, Baboushka was hard at work scrubbing her kitchen floor, when the doorbell rang. The noise was so unfamiliar to her that she froze in fright and sat for several minutes staring at the door. The bell rang again, stirring Baboushka out of her daze. She stood up, slowly walked over to the kitchen window and peeked outside to see three grand looking gentlemen standing on her doorstep.

Sensing that they meant no harm, she opened the door and greeted the three men, who were dressed in velvet robes and were wearing golden crowns.

'Good evening,' they said in unison. 'We three kings are on a long journey and need somewhere to rest for a while.'

Baboushka was so pleased to have some visitors that she welcomed them in without hesitation. She stoked the fire, set the table and warmed up some mulled wine and mince pies.

'We are extremely grateful for your hospitality,' said the first king.

'Where are you traveling to?' asked Baboushka.

'We are unsure of our destination,' replied the second king. 'We are following a bright star and hope that it will lead us to the birthplace of the holy child, baby Jesus.'

'Would you like to join us on our journey?' asked the third king.

Baboushka smiled. It was so kind of these gentlemen to invite her along with them on their journey. However, it would not be possible, she explained, because she had not yet finished cleaning her floor and besides, she had no gift for the baby. Perhaps next time.

Before long it was time for the three kings to leave. They thanked Baboushka again and tried once more to persuade her to join them, without success. She waved them off as they disappeared into the dark night.

The following morning Baboushka awoke and opened her curtains to see the forest had been covered in a blanket of white snow. She stoked the fire and sat down to a breakfast of muffins and jam before setting to work on her daily chores. Later that morning while polishing the living room furniture an overwhelming feeling of loneliness swept over her. She thought about the evening before and how wonderful it had felt to have the three kings sharing her mince pies. She thought about their journey and the newborn baby and felt sorry to have missed such a special event.

Baboushka suddenly stopped working. She ran to the closet and grabbed her winter coat, scarf, gloves and walking boots. She then dashed outside and picked a big thick sprig of holly covered in red berries. She would follow the path of the three kings and find the baby.

She set off, all the while scouring the sky for the bright star that the three kings had followed before her. Unable to find it, she decided to walk on through the day in the hope that it would reappear as night fell. However, that evening as the darkness drew in there was still no sign of it. Baboushka walked for days searching. The days turned in to weeks and the weeks turned into years, but still she could not find the star.

Legend has it that even to this day Baboushka is still searching and every Christmas she wraps up presents to give babies and children all over Russia in the hope that one day she will find the baby Jesus.

Adult-led activities to follow up the story

▶ Tell the story of the nativity – explain that Christmas is a Christian celebration and talk about what this means.

▶ Explore this festival and look at the associated traditions. Find out about different customs around the world.

▶ Ask the children to share their experiences of Christmas.

▶ Make Russian Christmas tree star ornaments. (Find an example on the Internet at **www.crayola.com/lesson-plans/detail/russian-star-ornaments-lesson-plan.**)

▶ Make star mobiles.

▶ Collaborate as a class to make a Christmas frieze. Allow the children to suggest their own ideas and provide a range of art resources for them to make their contributions.

▶ Play counting games using stars with different numbers of points. Divide the stars into triangles and challenge the children to count how many there are.

▶ Make stars using pentagons, hexagons and triangles.

Independent activities

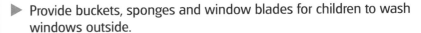

▶ Set up a small world nativity scene.

▶ Role-play a house with a variety of cleaning equipment and utensils.

▶ Provide buckets, sponges and window blades for children to wash windows outside.

▶ Provide Russian doll templates with a variety of patterns for painting and colouring.

▶ Print with Christmas sponge stencils in ready mixed paint.

▶ Make stars using card, glitter and silver and gold pens.

▶ Sort Russian dolls and arrange according to size.

Songs, rhymes and poems

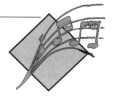

Silly Horse – by Vadim Levin and Evgeny Antonenkov.
A selection of Russian poems for children published by Pumpkin House Press.

Liuli, Liuli, Liuli
Find this Russian lullaby in Skip Across the Ocean published by Frances Lincoln.

Mama Lisa's World: Russia
Find a selection of children's songs and nursery rhymes in Russian and English script on the Internet at **www.mamalisa.com**

Links with the EYFS Areas of Learning and Development

PSED – Have a developing respect for their own cultures and beliefs and those of other people; be confident to speak in a familiar group; talk freely about their home and community.

CLL – Speak clearly and audibly with confidence and control and show an awareness of the listener.

PSRN – Count an irregular arrangement of objects; show an interest in shape by playing with shapes; use developing mathematical ideas and methods to solve practical problems.

KUW – Begin to know about their own cultures and beliefs and those of other people.

CD – Talk about personal intentions; work creatively on a large or small scale; create constructions, collages, paintings and drawings.

More stories and information

Baboushka by Arthur Scholey and Helen Cann – an illustrated retelling of the featured story.

Joy to the World: Christmas Stories from Around the Globe by Saviour Pirotta and Sheila Moxley – an illustrated collection including Baboushka.

Sasha and Babushka: A Story of Russia by Cornelia Evans, Vladimir Shpitalnik and Bella Krementsova – a little girl travels to Moscow to celebrate her birthday.

Russia ABCs: A Book about the People and Places of Russia by Ann Berge and Jeff Yesh – information book for young children.

Christmas Around the World by Anna Claybourne and Angelo Ruta – an illustrated information book about Christmas traditions in different countries.

Cbeebies Website for an animated version of the story Baboushka go to
www.bbc.co.uk/cbeebies/stories/world/baboushka.shtml

Sources

Elephant, Hare and Hippo – This tale originates from Southeast Africa. There are many variations and some stories feature a tortoise instead of a hare. The story in this book is an amalgamation of the various adaptations. Find one version in When Elephant was King and Other Elephant Tales from Africa (Struik Publishers, Johannesburg, 2000).

King Midas – This Ancient Greek myth dates back to the 8th Century. It was written by Roman poet Ovid and is one of a series of short stories that comprise his epic poem Metamorphoses (Oxford University Press, Oxford, 1998).

The Little Koala and the Bunyip – The bunyip is a creature of Aboriginal mythology dating back to the 1800s. It is often described as a lake monster that hides in Australian creeks and billabongs. Village storytellers tell young Aborigines bunyip stories at ceremonial gatherings or corroborees. The story in this book is sourced from The National Library of Australia website (**www.nla.gov.au**).

Paraparawa and Waraku – This creation myth comes from the Trio people from the Amazonian rainforests of Surinam and Brazil. The story is about how the spirit Waraku introduced the concept of farming and cultivation to the tribe. This story can be found in World Mythology: An Anthology of Great Myths and Epics by Donna Rosenberg (McGraw-Hill, Berkshire, 1993).

The Twelve Wild Geese –Irish oral story telling tradition that dates back hundreds of years. In the 19th century folklorist Pateick Kennedy transferred the story into print in his collection entitled The Fireside Stories of Ireland (M'Glashan And Gill, Dublin, 1870).

Qasiagssaq, The Great Liar – This moral tale comes from the North American Inuit tribes of Alaska. Variations of this story can be found using the alternative spelling of Kasiagsak. The story in this book was sourced from Stories from Native North America by Linda Raczek (Wayland, Sussex, 2000).

The Partridge and the Fox – Author and collector of fairy tales, Henri Pourrat, transcribed this folktale from Auvergne in France during the late 19th Century. Pourrat's version can be found on the Internet on a website dedicated to his works (**www.henripourrat.com**).

Cat, Dog and Monkey – This is a folktale from Java in Indonesia. It is difficult to find in print but one version can be found in South & North, East & West by Michael Rosen (Walker Books, London, 1992).

The Monkey's Heart – This story from India is recorded in the Panchatantra – a collection of Hindu and Buddhist fables, dating back to 200 BC. It is sometimes entitled The Monkey and the Crocodile or The Monkey and Alghlim. Find an illustrated version in Stories from India by Anna Milbourne and Linda Edwards (Usborne, London, 2004).

The Lion and the Nien – Although the lion is not native to China, it has been a part of Chinese folklore for many centuries. The story in this book is associated with Chinese New Year and explains why the lion is traditionally regarded as a protector from evil spirits. Although there are many different versions of this story, the main source for this book was The Lion Dance in Stories from China by Saviour Pirotta (Wayland, Sussex, 1999).

Anansi and the Box of Stories – Anansi stories originate from the oral tradition of the Ashanti tribe in Ghana, West Africa. The African people took them to the Caribbean, where more tales were born. A large number of Anansi stories are now in print and these may also be found using the alternative spellings of Ananse, Anancy and Kweku Ananse. This story has many different versions, but the account in this book is based on Pat Perrin's version published on the Internet at **www.chironbooks.com/NovelsforYoungReaders.html**.

The Rat's Wedding – This story originates from the Punjab region between Pakistan and India. Sometimes told as The Long-tailed Rat or The Rat Who Made One Bargain Too Many, it is a moral tale about a rat that pushes his luck too far. The version in this book is mainly sourced from Tales of the Punjab by Flora Annie Steel (Macmillan, London, 1894).

The Dragon of Krakow – This famous legend tells of the Dragon of Wawel Hill in Krakow, Poland. The dragon is now the symbol of this city. Many versions of the story can be found both in print and on the Internet. The one in this book can be found in Old Polish Legends by F.C. Anstruther and J. Sekalski (Hippocrene Books, New York, 1991).

The Spell-bound Giant – There are few Portuguese folk tales in print, especially in contemporary forms. This tale was found in Portuguese Folk-Tales by Consiglieri Pedroso, translated by Henrietta Monteiro (Folk Lore Society Publications, New York 1882).

Baboushka – This well-known 19th Century Christmas tale is sometimes described as a Russian version of the St Nicholas story. The story in this book was originally sourced from Rainbow Year by Moira Andrew, Robyn Gordon and Andrea Heath (Belair Publications, Bedfordshire, 1994). However, it has been substantially adapted to take various other versions into account.

Resources

TTS Group
www.tts-group.co.uk
0800 318686

General resources: Nursery rhyme figures and finger puppets; bark chippings; soap flakes; food colouring; cellophane; glitter; pipe cleaners; lolly sticks; feathers; wiggly eyes; sequins; clay; Chinese New Year figure set; BeeBot and alphabet mat; height chart; water cascade set.

Role-play/small world: Nursery rhyme, arctic and jungle active worlds mats; arctic animal set; gem stones; rainforest animal set; instant snow powder; snakes; magic microphone; Punjabi and sari outfits; multicultural food; castle; Eskimo house; people of the world figures; Duplo world people; vacuum cleaner; iron.

Games/puzzles: Nursery rhyme jigsaws; Cheeky Chimps literacy activities; rhyming objects; dog and puppy numeracy set; sorting gems in treasure chest; elephant jigsaws.

Early Learning Centre
www.elc.co.uk
08705 352352

General resources: Play tents and tunnels; tape measure; adventure bug kit; illuminated globe; musical instruments.

Role-play/small world: Cleaning trolley; castles; knights; jungle adventure crocodile and elephant; microphones.

Games/puzzles: Travel the world; Puff pop up dragon; Hungry hippos; Globe trotting; Castle puzzle; Monster puzzle.

Orchard Toys
www.orchardtoys.com
01953 859520

Games: Magic cauldron; King of the castle; Insey wincey spider; Wild world lotto; Jelly elephants; Spotty dogs.

Puzzles: World map; Magical castle; Who's in the jungle?

Playmobil
www.playmobil.com
01268 490184

Small world: Magic castle and royal characters; goldmine; zoo animals; knights and castle; magician's workshop.

Amazon
www.amazon.co.uk

You will find all the books mentioned in this Little Book on Amazon.

Storybooks

The Great Tug of War: And Other Stories **by Beverley Naidoo and Piet Grobler**

Tales of Wisdom and Wonder **by Hugh Lupton and Niamh Sharkey**

Usborne Illustrated Stories from Around the World **by Heather Amery and Linda Edwards**

The Kingfisher Treasury of Stories from Around the World **by Linda Jennings and Victor Ambrus**

A Twist in the Tale: Animal Stories from Around the World **by Mary Hoffman and Jan Ormerod**

The Whistling Monster: Stories from Around the World **by Jamila Gavin**

North & South, East & West: 25 Stories from Around the World **by Michael Rosen**

The Barefoot Book of Animal Tales from Around the World **by Naomi Adler and Amanda Hall**

Talk with Me! and Walk with Me! **by Sheila Blackstone and Caroline Mockford**

Usborne Stories from India **by Anna Milbourne and Linda Edwards.**

Sing Me a Story! Song and Dance Stories from the Caribbean **by Grace Hallworth and John Clementson**

The Fabrics of Fairytale: Stories spun from far and wide **by Tanya Robyn Batt and Rachel Griffin**

Information Books

My Multicultural Atlas **by Benoit Delalandre and Jeremy Clapin**

Get Dressed **by Gwenyth Swain**

Global Babies **by the Global Fund for Children**

Playtime Around the World and Home Around the World **by Kate Petty in association with Oxfam**

Traditional Folk Costumes of Europe: Paper Dolls in Full Costume **by Kathy Allert**

All Kinds of Beliefs by Emma Damon

Activity Books

Sparklers Polar Workout, Desert Workout, Rainforest Workout and Underwater Workout (four books) – **published by Evans Books (www.evansbooks.co.uk)**

Websites

World Info Zone – **www.worldinfozone.com**

BBC News Country Profiles
– **http://news.bbc.co.uk/1/hi/country_profiles/default.stm**

Oxfam Education – **www.oxfam.org.uk/education/resources**

More Information ──────────────────

Research Reports

Independent Review of the Teaching of Early Reading: Final Report (Rose Review), 2006, DfES Publications, Nottingham
(available from: **www.standards.dfes.gov.uk/phonics/rosereview**)

Every Child a Talker: Guidance for Early Language Lead Practitioners, 2008, DfES Publications, Nottingham
(available from: **http://nationalstrategies.standards.dcsf.gov.uk/node/153355**)

Effective Provision of Pre-school Education: Final Report, 2004, DfES Publications, Nottingham (available from: **www.dcsf.gov.uk/everychildmatters/research/keyresearch/eppe/eppe**)

Books

Foundations of Literacy, Sue Palmer and Ros Bayley, 2004, Network Educational Press (tel: 01202 665432 – website: **www.networkcontinuum.co.uk**)

The Little Book of Storytelling, Mary Medlicott, 2003, Featherstone Education (tel: 0207 758 0200 - website: **www.acblack.com/featherstone**)

Communication, Language and Literacy from Birth to Five, Avril Brock and Carolynn Rankin, 2008, Sage Publications (tel: 0207 324 8500 – **website: www.uk.sagepub.com**)

Websites

National Literacy Trust – **www.literacytrust.org.uk**

Every Child Matters – **www.dcsf.gov.uk/everychildmatters**

Department for Children Schools and Families –
www.nationalstrategies.standards.dcsf.gov.uk/earlyyears